D1480696

COINS
AND
CHRISTIANITY

KENNETH A. JACOB

LONDON

DEDICATION

The revised and enlarged edition of *Coins and Christianity* I dedicate to the memory of my wife, Eileen Winifred, with gratitude for her tolerance in allowing me to 'play with my toys (coins)' and for everything.

© 1985 Kenneth A. Jacob
2nd edition, revised and enlarged, published 1985
First published 1959

Published by B. A. Seaby Ltd, 8 Cavendish Square, London W1M 0AJ

Distributed on behalf of
B. A. Seaby Ltd
by
B. T. Batsford Ltd
P.O. Box 4, Braintree, Essex CM7 7QY, England

ISBN 0 900652 73 X

Typeset by Pardy & Son (Printers) Ltd, Parkside, Ringwood, Hampshire and printed in Great Britain by R. J. Acford, Chichester, Sussex.

CONTENTS

PREFACE

This book is about coins – but it is written for the general
reader rather than for the coin collector or student, numismatists as we are called.

Thirty years ago I prepared and read to the Cambridgeshire
Numismatic Society, a paper entitled 'Coins and Christianity'.
This paper was kindly received by my fellow members and the
title evoked considerable comment from others who had no
interest in coins. These comments prompted me to write this
book which, although based to some extent upon the paper
mentioned, was planned with rather a different end in view and
in different presentation.

In the first chapter I have tried to provide the background for
a brief consideration of the coins of the Bible. Then, from
Roman times during which Christian references on coins are
first to be found, to trace the story of the growth of the
coinages through the centuries to the present day with particular reference throughout to the many ways in which Christianity and the Christian Church have been linked with the
coinage. Whether I have succeeded in this undertaking is not
for me to say, but I have gained much pleasure, knowledge,
and interest in making the attempt.

From the sixth century BC to the present day, with the
products of one mint or another, we are presented with an

unbroken line of coinages, and numismatists of the past and present have provided us with a very complete knowledge of the coins of all periods. Although there is very much definite fact known, there are many problems still to be solved, controversial matters to be agreed, and uncertainties to be turned into sureties. Fresh discoveries of single coins or hoards, and new theories (frequently controversial), evolved by students, keep the state of numismatic knowledge moving slowly towards a complete understanding and, in the light of such advances, theories and suggestions formerly accepted have sometimes to be abandoned. It is most likely that the future will put different interpretations upon a few of the points stated here as facts (I am fully aware that some are not generally accepted), but until definite proof to the contrary is forthcoming, I feel it quite in order to leave these debatable facts as they stand without comment.

The numismatic facts gathered together are almost all readily accessible in the many and various works available for study. It is with sincere gratitude that I acknowledge my debt to the many authors whose works I have consulted, and a list of the books most frequently used is published. From these, fuller and further information on many matters connected with this book can be sought, but in view of the nature of the book I have not felt it necessary to add complete footnote references for all my statements. In this new edition of *Coins and Christianity* I have attempted to take account of the relevant studies which have appeared in recent years.

It is my pleasant duty to thank many friends who have given me their opinion on a number of points of detail and who have encouraged me in this study. Where, in a very few instances, I have not followed the suggestions offered, the responsibility is, of course, my own. Those who have helped me are too numerous to mention by name, but I should like particularly to thank my friend Mr Frank S. Snow, who read the greater part of the manuscript of the first edition of this book and who made many valuable comments.

Although I might well have been able to employ finer specimens, as far as has been possible I have used my own coins for the illustrations. I have adopted this plan deliberately in order that the point might be made clear that a very ordinary person such as myself can own specimens of some of the pieces mentioned. Coin collecting is not the hobby only of the very rich or very learned – anyone with a desire can acquire for a fairly modest outlay just a few pieces of historical interest and from which considerable delight can be obtained.

There are several gaps in the coins I wished to illustrate which my own collection could not fill and it is with gratitude that I record my thanks to the Keepers of the Departments of Coins and Medals in the British Museum, London, the Fitz-william Museum, Cambridge, the Hunterian Museum, Glas-gow, and the Ashmolean Museum, Oxford, for allowing the illustration of coins in their collections. Similarly to the owners of a few pieces from other private collections.

My thanks are also due to Mr P. Frank Purvey for the photographing of the coins for the illustration, to Miss Wendy Fraser for typing the manuscript, and last, but by no means least, to Mr Peter A. Clayton (Publications Director of B.A. Seaby Ltd.) for the expert help and advice given so freely and for the manner in which he has guided this book through the press.

Finally, may I say that no attempt has been made to intro-duce Christian propaganda in the book. If the reader wishes to peruse the text with this in mind, it could well be done, and a list of the Biblical references mentioned is given. I hope the reader may find here an interpretation of some facts about coins and Christianity which might otherwise have remained unknown or obscure.

May 1985   K.A.J.
                                        Elmbridge
                                        Cranleigh

NOTE: All coins are illustrated at actual size unless otherwise noted.

1

THE SCENE IS SET

Considered purely from the historical standpoint, there can be little doubt about the earthly life of Jesus of Nazareth. Although no undoubted archaeological evidence of His life has been discovered, the effects of it are evident in the pattern of history through the centuries, and they have done much to formulate the basis of the lives of many peoples of the world in the present day. Possibly the most commonplace example of this springs readily to mind. Jesus has been aptly described as 'The Man who broke history in two' as our era is dated from His birth, although, to be strictly accurate, the actual date of the Nativity was almost certainly in or just before the year known to us as 4 BC, in which year the death of Herod the Great took place. Christianity has also had considerable effect in one form or another upon many of the world's coinages down to the present day, and a consideration of these provides the object of this book.

Coins have a many sided interest to those who study or collect them – their use; their art; their designs (or types, as they are known to the numismatist); their connection with peoples, individuals, or places of the past or present. To impress the reality of Biblical happenings upon the mind of the ordinary person, possibly nothing better can be done than to visit the sites of the ancient cities in which these events actually took place. It is, however, given to few to have this privilege, but it is open to many to handle – even to own – a coin struck and used in the ancient cities, as they are probably the most numerous of antiquarian objects which have survived and which, in some cases, can be purchased for a modest outlay. It is possible to possess coins of the cities to the inhabitants of which St Paul addressed his epistles – Colossae, Corinth, Ephesus, Philippi, Rome, Thessalonica – or many other cities which are mentioned in the Bible; for example, places visited by St Paul in his travels such as Amphipolis (Acts 17:1), Melita (Malta) (Acts 28:1), and Syracuse (Acts 28:12), or the Seven Churches in Revelation 1:11: Ephesus, Smyrna, Pergamum, Thyatira, Sardis, Philadelphia, and Laodiceia. Such coins can give an added sense of reality and tangible evidence to the written accounts.

The Greeks in Lydia in Asia Minor were responsible for the invention of coinage about, or not long after, 640 BC. The Greek series of coins was later superseded by the Roman, and this in turn gave way to the Byzantine and various European coinages which have, in some cases, been maintained to the present day. Accordingly, from the time of the invention of coinage there has been an unbroken line issued by one authority or another spanning about twenty-six centuries. The Lydian coins were struck in electrum (an alloy of gold and silver) and the royal badge, the forepart of a lion, appeared as the type shown on them. The invention of coinage was soon copied in Greece itself at Aegina where the coins were struck in silver, the type being a turtle. Possibly by about 570 BC coinages were beginning to be established in Corinth and about 560 in Athens, and these were closely followed by others. The ancient Greek world was composed of many city states – not always friendly disposed towards one another – and from the early beginnings many cities, and even some small village communities, very soon began to issue their own coinage, marking and distinguishing it by the employment of types of local significance. These many coinages were, in most cases, contemporary with one another. Many of the coins are inscribed with the name of the place of mintage, either in full or in abbreviated form. As an example, the coins of Athens are normally inscribed AΘE, which are the first three letters of the name of the city and which would imply 'a coin of Athens'. The words 'a coin' do not actually appear, but would have been understood by the users.

The coins of ancient Greece include some of the finest known examples of numismatic art and many are prized by collectors for this reason if for no other, large numbers being in absolutely perfect condition of preservation in spite of their great age.

In the earliest coinages the types generally employed were in all probability of a secular nature, but there is full evidence that before long many types were of a religious character and connection. Representations of gods and goddesses appeared on Greek coins from early times, but apart from two or three possible minor exceptions, the first human portrait to appear on a coin was that of Alexander the Great. Even so, on the coins struck by Ptolemy I of Egypt and Lysimachus of Thrace which employ the portrait of Alexander as the type, he is shown deified after his death with the horn of Ammon on his brow (cf. Daniel 8:21). Ptolemy later took the next step as he issued coins bearing his own portrait and during his lifetime, the date of the innovation being about 300 BC; this precedent has remained a feature of many of the world's coinages.

Archaeological evidence shows that from the most primitive time some form of religious belief has formed a part of the make up of mankind, whether it be a polytheistic conception such as those of the ancient Egyptians, Greeks, and Romans, or a monotheistic conception of the Jews, Christians and Muslims with the one supreme Being. In any consideration of such different religions and with the present subject specially in mind, it should be remembered that in the imagination of the ancient peoples their gods and goddesses were for them reality, and must have meant quite as much to them at the time, and in their own ways, as Christ does to the Christian of the present day or as Allah does to the Muslim. Consider for example the funeral rites of the ancient Egyptian: his elaborate processes of mummification; his extensive tombs with furniture and utensils, and all other preparations made to support his belief of the return of the spirit to the body from which it had departed. Would the ancient Egyptian have gone to all this trouble if he had not a firm belief that what he was doing was right for the deceased; and may he not have gained quite as much help and comfort for himself in the passing of a loved one as does the follower of Christ in his Christian ritual?

With this point in mind it is easy to see that a religious motif had a very real significance to the peoples of the past when employed as a coin type. The coin would become an object of some reverence apart from its utilitarian purpose; and who would dare deface or mutilate that which portrayed the image of the local diety or some object associated with the cult? The essential characteristics of a coin are that it is made from metal of intrinsic (or token) value; it is of an agreed weight, and is marked in some manner as a guarantee by the issuing authority. Therefore, a religious motif or type would signify also that the issuer must of necessity strike a coin of good metal and weight – he dare not do otherwise and mark his coin with such a type. A further reason for the employment of religious types on many coins may also be found in the fact that ancient temples were frequently used as storage places for treasure. It must be remembered that the temples of the Greeks were not places of worship or sacrifice but were, in fact, considered as the home of the god or goddess to whom the temple was dedicated. In the most basic form the temple consisted of the *cella*, or room within which stood a statue of the diety, with a porch before it. In the more elaborate temples behind the *cella* was another chamber in which the treasures dedicated to the deity would be stored and the place where the coins might well have been struck.

The coins were usually made by the preparation of a small metal pellet or disc cut or cast to the agreed and required weight. This blank, as it is called, was then placed on a die, usually made of iron, bronze or steel, on the upper surface of which the design to be reproduced on the coin had been engraved in recess (intaglio). On the upper surface of the blank a punch was rested, and two or three blows from a hammer or mallet on the upper end of the punch would force it into the metal of the blank which, in turn, would force the lower surface of the blank into the recesses of the engraved die. The punch in the earliest times was without specific form, but this soon developed so as to impress a definite pattern or design on the coin. The next development was the punch taking the form of an engraved die similar to the engraved lower die, and thus designs were impressed on both sides of the coin. This hammered method of striking coins remained in use until the sixteenth century AD when machinery to assist in the striking process was first employed, and which gradually replaced the earlier method.

From primitive beginnings the Greek coinage developed in style, and with improved technique in the engraving of the dies reached a high degree of perfection in the fifth and fourth centuries BC – a perfection possibly never equalled even to modern times – but it tended to wane in the Hellenistic period. As the influence of Rome became more evident and the Roman empire spread its boundaries, the Roman tradition of coinage engulfed the Greek.

Greek silver coins were based mainly upon the drachm which varied in weight to a considerable extent according to the standard employed by the particular mint at which the coin was struck. Multiples of two, four, eight, and ten drachms were used at times, but the pieces of two and four drachms (the didrachm and tetradrachm) were the most usual. Fractions of the drachm to the obol, which was the sixth part, were used, also the half obol appeared at times and, rarely, fractions down to the eighth-obol which was a tiny coin little bigger than the head of a large pin and called a hemitartemorion. Gold and electrum (an alloy of gold and silver) were used on occasions (drachms of gold are mentioned in Ezra 2:69) and bronze was employed largely from the fourth century BC. The name 'stater' which is frequently applied to Greek silver coins signifies the 'standard' coin of the particular mint rather than a specific denomination. It so happens that the standard coin is often equivalent to the didrachm (two drachms), but at some mints it equals other denominations e.g. Corinth, three drachms, and in the Jewish series where it is known as the shekel, four drachms (a tetradrachm). Although the names of several denominations of Greek bronze coins are known, it is only in a very few instances that a particular coin can now be known to be of one denomination or another, and it is customary for numismatists to refer to them by their diameter.

Although the Greek coinage had been introduced in the seventh century BC and had been used in the Greek colonies in Italy from the sixth century, the coinage of Rome itself was commenced at a very much later date. The first Roman currency was in the form of lumps of bronze completely unworked and known as *aes rude* and may date from the fifth century BC. In the first quarter of the third century heavy bronze bars with varied types were used, but these *aes signatum* were money and not coin as they were not adjusted to a correct weight and had to be weighed at every transaction. About the same time cast coins of bronze were produced but the exact date of their introduction is still debated by students. The heavy weight standards of these first coins – *aes grave* – were reduced by stages and eventually gave way to smaller and lighter struck coins. The standard coin was the *as*, the Roman pound of bronze, but multiples and fractions of the *as* were also used. Silver coins based on the contemporary Greek coinages of cities in South Italy were introduced by the Romans in the third century, no doubt mainly for the purpose of trading with these Greek cities, but a big innovation followed perhaps about 212 BC (a date also much debated). This was the introduction of a new silver coin known as the denarius, intended for use in Rome itself. The denarius weighed at first about 70 grains but it was reduced some thirty years later to about 61 grains, and was thus somewhat similar to the Greek drachm.

The denarius was tariffed at first as equal to 10 *asses* but was later revalued at 16 *asses* and it remained the mainstay of the Roman coinage throughout the Republic. A denarius of gold, the aureus (valued at 25 silver denarii) was struck at times, but the bronze coinage was little used during the first century BC. A reform undertaken by Augustus, the first Roman emperor (27 BC–AD 14), continued the use of the denarius as the principal coin and it remained tariffed at 16 *asses*. The gold aureus also appeared, and lower denominations in base metal consisted of the *as* (**1**) struck in copper and pieces of two and four *asses*, the dupondius and sestertius, usually struck in orichalcum (an alloy of copper and zinc). Occasional fractions of the *as* also appeared. The sestertius (**26**), a fine large coin, is greatly prized by collectors and fortunately in many reigns is reasonably plentiful to this day. A gradual debasement of the quality of the silver of the denarius and weight reductions led to some alterations in the coinage system in the second and third centuries AD and the sestertius dropped out of use. A further reform undertaken by Diocletian about AD 294 set the Roman coinage on a pattern which lasted, although with some change, mainly in weight reductions, until the fall of the empire in the West in AD 476. The later coinage was mainly of bronze with a small number of gold coins, but silver was rarely used.

1   Copper *as* of Nero (AD 54–68) with the emperor's name and titles on the obverse and a winged Victory on the reverse holding a shield inscribed SPQR (= The Senate and People of Rome).

As in the case of the Greek coinages, portraits of the Roman deities had been used regularly as coin types, but the first Roman coin to carry a portrait of a living person was that of Julius Caesar, denarii with his portrait appearing in 44 BC, the year of his assassination. From the time of Augustus the portrait of the emperor (**19**) formed the normal type on the obverse of the coins (the obverse being the main side of the coin), and many dies were exceptionally finely engraved. The resultant portraits are often outstandingly attractive and, accordingly, the collector can gather together a fascinating group of the successive emperors. Reference to these portraits will be made later.

The coinage of Rome had, in general, a far greater degree of centralization than the Greek as it was used throughout the whole of the empire. Certain Greek cities, however, were permitted a degree of autonomy by the Romans in the matter of coinage and at times were allowed to strike coins (mainly of bronze and for local use) but this privilege was withdrawn from the last of them, Alexandria, with the monetary reform of Diocletian. These autonomous issues of the Roman period are known to numismatists as the 'Greek Imperial' series, and although many of the coins bear the portrait of the reigning emperor of Rome as the normal type on the obverse, most retain something of their Greek character and the inscriptions on the coins are frequently in Greek. Thus, there are known to us coinages of many cities mentioned in the Bible such as Antioch and Athens which have their beginnings in the Greek series proper and which close in the Greek Imperial series.

Attention can now be turned to the lands of the eastern Mediterranean area and in particular to the coins of the Jews, to provide the background to the coinage in use in Palestine during the lifetime of Jesus and to the coins of the Bible.

Under Croesus, who became king of Lydia about 564 BC, a coinage had been established, first in electrum and then in gold and silver. The earliest coins show the foreparts of a lion and bull back to back, but the later issues depict them facing each other; a rough punch mark appearing on the reverse of them all. In 546 BC the Persians captured Lydia and it appears probable that they continued striking coins in the Lydian types until about 510 BC (*Num. Chron.* 1961, p. 115) when a new coinage was first introduced which consisted of gold darics and silver sigloi (**2**). These coins depict the Great King himself as a half-length figure, either shooting with a bow and arrow or running with a bow and arrow or a dagger. The rough punch

2   Persian silver sigloi of the fourth century BC with the figure
of the Great King holding a dagger and a rough punch mark on
the reverse.

mark was continued on the reverse. Coins of these types were
struck by the Persians over a long period of time and, as they
are uninscribed, it is difficult to attribute them to the actual
kings who issued them.

Although coinage had been invented shortly before the fall
of Jerusalem to the Babylonians and the deportation of the Jews
to Babylon which commenced in 597 BC, it is unlikely that
they had much if any contact with coins during the captivity.
The Babylonian empire was brought to an end by the fall of
Babylon to the Persian king Cyrus in 539 BC. In the following
year an edict was issued by him (Ezra 1:1) which allowed the
Jews to return to their homeland and it also decreed that the
'house of God at Jerusalem be built', a task probably completed
in 516 BC.

There is little doubt that as Judah was a province of the
Persian empire following the return from exile, the Persian
darics and sigloi would have been known and circulated
amongst the Jews until the Greek conquest of the land under
Alexander the Great. Coins from Greek cities were in circulation in the area, being brought in during the course of trading.
In particular, the coins of Athens had become widely known,
used and accepted, so much so that copies of them began to be
made in various places for local use. A very few small coins
struck in silver are known which were probably minted in the
mid-fourth century BC. Although of extreme rarity, several
different types are found on these coins including a copy of the
Athenian owl; a bird which has been identified almost certainly
as a falcon, and a lily, a flower commonly found in ancient
times and noted for its scent and elegance (Luke 12:27). Some
of these coins are inscribed in ancient Hebrew characters YHD =

JEHUD = JUDAH and accordingly it would appear certain they were issued by a Jewish authority and probably struck in Jerusalem.

Another coin of interest was struck during the Persian period, probably in the Philistinian city of Gaza (**3**) which is mentioned in the Bible in connection with the story of Samson (Judges 16:1). This extremely rare coin has on the obverse the bearded and helmeted head of a man and, on the reverse, a figure of a man, similarly bearded, seated on a winged wheel holding on his outstretched left hand a bird variously described as a hawk or falcon. Once again this coin is inscribed YHD, but it is in Aramaic and not the ancient Hebrew script and it is of

3   Silver coin probably struck at the Philistine city of Gaza. On the obverse is the bearded and helmeted head of a man and the reverse has a figure seated on a winged wheel. The inscription reads YHD. (Enlarged to twice actual size.)

larger size and about ten times the weight of the other YHD coins mentioned. The unusual reverse type has given rise to considerable discussion and speculation on account of the similarity in conception with the vision of Ezekiel with the wings and wheels (Ezekiel 1:4ff., and 3:13). It has also been suggested the inscription should be read as YHW (= Yahweh) and, accordingly, that it is the Jehovah of the Old Testament whose figure is represented on the coin – a 'still small voice among the kings and satraps, the heroes and Olympians', as it has been described. In front of the seated figure and facing it, is an object which has been noted as a bald-headed and bearded mask. Although the significance of this remains uncertain, a

suggestion has been made by M. Wacks that it is a representation of Ezekiel himself, reference being made to Ezekiel 1:28.
Although struck perhaps about the same time as the other YHD
coins, the larger size and heavier weight and the Aramaic
inscription would point to a different issuing authority –
probably the Persian authorities themselves. The problem is
perhaps best resolved in the words of Y. Meshorer in his
important study of the series *Jewish Coins of the Second Temple
Period*, p. 37f:

> If our suggestion is adopted that only the minute coins were
> minted by the Jews, whereas the larger one was struck by the
> Persian authorities themselves, this design would be construed in
> terms of a representation of God as the Persians pictured Him. We
> thus have depicted here the Divinity worshipped by the Jewish
> population as interpreted by the Persians, a customary procedure
> of theirs in other parts, too, of their great empire.

Some degree of a unified coinage was evident when the
confederation of Greek states, led by Alexander the Great of
Macedon (336–323 BC), entered Asia Minor in 334. He was
victorious over the Persians in battles at the Granicus river and
at Issus, extending the Greek empire through Palestine, down
into Egypt and, after the decisive victory over the Persians
at Gaugamela in 331, on to the east as far as northern India.
Alexander's progress south through Palestine was delayed by
the Phoenician city of Tyre resisting the advance but, following a seven-month siege, it paid for delaying the Greeks by
being destroyed. On the other hand, according to the Jewish
historian Josephus who wrote in the first century AD, when
Alexander actually visited Jerusalem he was welcomed by the
priests and impressed by their piety; accordingly he endowed
the city with extraordinary privileges.

Throughout his vast empire Alexander's coins were widely
circulated. For the types on the gold coins he depicted the
goddess Athena on the obverse and Victory on the reverse; on
his silver coins (**4**), the head of young Herakles wearing the
lion's skin on the obverse, and Zeus seated on a throne holding
his eagle on the reverse. These coins were struck at many mints

4 Silver tetradrachm of Alexander the Great (336–323 BC) struck at Damascus (Acts 9:13) *c.* 330–319 BC, with the head of young Herakles on the obverse and Zeus enthroned on the reverse.

throughout the empire including Tarsus (Acts 21:39), Damascus (Acts 9:2), Babylon (Daniel 1:1), Tyre and Sidon (Matthew 15:21), and Ake (Judges 1:31).

After Alexander's death his empire was divided into smaller portions and Palestine became part of the Egyptian kingdom ruled by Ptolemy I and his successors and Egyptian coins would have circulated in place of Alexander's. By 198 BC Egyptian rule was finally overcome in Palestine by Antiochus III of Syria (222–187 BC) and the coins of the Seleucid empire replaced the Egyptian coins, although many of the other pieces would still be in circulation and known. During the period of the Seleucid rule in Palestine their introduction of Greek customs and their forbidding of the Jews following their religion (which included the desecration of the Temple in Jerusalem by Antiochus IV), led to the rebellion of the Jews in 167 BC. With Judas Maccabaeus as their leader they liberated Jerusalem in 164 BC, but in a decisive battle not far from Bethlehem which followed soon afterwards, they were defeated. However, one object of the rebellion was achieved as favourable peace terms were offered, with liberty of worship being granted and, after further effort, political independence from the Syrians followed in 142 BC.

Peace being established again, Antiochus VII (138–129 BC) (**5**) gave a grant to the Jewish high-priest, Simon Maccabaeus, in 138 BC giving him leave 'to coin money for thy country with thine own stamp' (1 Maccabees 15:6). It appears, however, that no coins were actually struck under the grant as

5 Silver tetradrachm with a portrait of Antiochus VII (138–129 BC), the Syrian King who granted coining rights to Simon Maccabeus.

it was only a short time afterwards that this state of accord was broken, as is evident from later in the same chapter (Maccabees 15:27f.). The coins which have in the past been attributed to Simon Maccabaeus have now all been re-attributed to the period of the First Revolt of the Jews against Rome, AD 66–70.

Apart from the very rare silver coins mentioned above which were struck by or for the Jews in the Persian period, their first regular coinage consisted of small bronze pieces known as prutoth (singular: prutah) which were struck by later descendants of Simon Maccabaeus; the dynasty being known as the Hasmonaeans following the name of an ancestor. These coins are usually poorly struck and badly preserved (**6**); they frequently have as the obverse type an inscription within a wreath and, on the reverse, two cornucopiae with a poppy-head between them. This inscription is written in ancient Hebrew script and translated reads: 'Jehochanan the High Priest and the Community of the Jews'. Once again difficulty has been experienced in the attribution and dating of these coins as the same Hebrew names of the high priests are

6 Typical Jewish copper prutoth of the first century BC with an inscription within a wreath and double cornucopiae (horns of plenty).

encountered in different generations of the priestly family. It has been a matter of considerable debate to decide exactly which individual was responsible for the striking of the coins and whose name appeared on them. Apparently this problem has now been solved by the researches of Y. Meshorer mentioned below. The cornucopiae were no doubt copied from the coins of the Ptolemies and Seleucids which were used by the Jews whilst under their domination since the division of Alexander's Greek empire.

One series of the coins of this period varies from the normal types as just described. Of these, two varieties are known, one of which depicts on the obverse a flower, probably a lily, and the coin is inscribed in ancient Hebrew characters 'Jehonatan the King' (**7**). On the reverse is an anchor, presumably copied from that which appeared on many coins of the kings of Syria, together with the inscription in Greek ΒΑΣΙΛΕΩΣ ΑΛΕΞΑΝ-ΔΡΟΥ ('of Alexander the king'). The inscriptions become intelligible when it is realized that at the time the high priests were considered more or less as kings, and Alexander Janneaus (103–76 BC) actually assumed kingship at the commencement of his reign: this he claims on his coins, Alexander and Jehonatan being his Greek and Hebrew names.

7   Bronze prutah of Alexander Jannaeus (103–76 BC) with flower and anchor types.

The second variety of these coins has the anchor on the obverse with a Greek inscription (**8**), and on the reverse the Hebrew inscription set within the rays of a star or the spokes of a wheel. With the Second Commandment in mind the wheel would seem to be more probable than the star. Alexander Janneaus also struck coins of the normal types with the Hebrew inscription in a wreath and the double cornucopiae; Meshorer suggests his coins inaugurate the Hasmonaean series. Earlier

8 Bronze prutah of Alexander Jannaeus (103–76 BC) with anchor and wheel or star types.

students have attributed the first issues to John Hyrcanus I (135–104 BC), but Meshorer provides good argument to support his attributions and his dating would seem to be correct, the coins that were previously attributed to John Hyrcanus I now being given to John Hyrcanus II (63–40 BC).

A few coins of smaller size were struck at times, half-prutoth, but coins larger than the prutah appeared when Antigonus Mattathais was high priest (40–37 BC), both his Greek and Hebrew names being shown on his coins. His smaller coins introduce a variation of types as the seven-branched candlestick and showbread table are depicted. The coins of the Hasmonaean series concluded when Herod the Great became king under Roman influence in 37 BC.

The coins of Herod the Great (37–4 BC) and later members of his family were all struck in bronze and all the inscriptions are in Greek. Herod is well known from his connection with the story of the Nativity (Matthew 2:3, etc.) and his coins were inscribed with his name ΗΡΩΔΟΥ ΒΑΣΙΛΕΩΣ ('of Herod the king'). The types are varied and include a sacrificial tripod, caduceus, pomegranate, palm, wreath, and an uncertain object which may be a helmet (**9**). Herod was an Idumaean and not a Jew and few of his types are of Jewish significance.

9 Bronze coin of Herod the Great (37–4 BC) with a tripod and what may be an ornamented helmet.

Following the death of Herod, his kingdom was divided amongst his sons and Herod Archelaus (4 BC–AD 6), who is mentioned in Matthew 2:22, ruled over Judaea, Samaria, and Idumaea, and was given the title of Ethnarch (Governor of the People) by the Romans. The title appears on the coins together with his name HPωΔOY EΘNAPXOY and his types include the double cornucopiae, the anchor, the prow of a galley, a bunch of grapes and a crested helmet (**10**). Herod Antipas (4 BC–AD 39) was given the title of Tetrarch, ruler of a fourth part which consisted of Galilee and Peraea. It was Antipas who had St John the Baptist beheaded (Matthew 14:1) and who was

10   Bronze coin of Herod Archelaus (4 BC–AD 6) with a bunch of grapes and a crested helmet.

described by Jesus as 'that fox' (Luke 13:32), and to whom He was sent by Pontius Pilatus during His trial when Pilatus learnt that Jesus was a Galilaean (Luke 23:7). It would seem that Antipas struck no coins until the twenty-fourth year of his reign; this is evident as his coins are all dated by his regnal years and none are known of earlier dates. The coins are all rare and of those which are known the types include a palm branch, a reed, and a bunch of dates, together with the inscription HPWΔOY TETPAPXOY.

The coins of Herod Agrippa I (AD 37–44), who had St James put to death by the sword and who imprisoned St Peter (Acts 12:2 and 4), are inscribed BACIΛEWC AΓPIΠΠA and the types include a canopy coupled with, on the reverse, three ears of barley (**11**). A new feature of his coins is that his portrait is shown on some of them and also, on a few, portraits of the Roman emperors Caligula and Claudius. The Herodian king to complete those to be mentioned is Agrippa II (AD 56–95) before whom St Paul pleaded (Acts 26:1). Once again, his portrait is shown and also some of the Roman emperors.

11   Bronze coin of Herod Agrippa (AD 37–44) with a canopy and three ears of barley.

After Herod Archelaus was banished by the Romans in AD 6, they appointed procurators in his place to govern Judaea, Samaria, and Idumaea, who in turn issued a series of bronze coins. These are of small size somewhat similar to the earlier prutoth, frequently showing the names and the regnal years of the Roman emperors. There was a brief interval when parts of these territories were returned to the rule of Herod Agrippa I in AD 41 until his death three years later. The coins of the procurators finally conclude with the rebellion of the Jews against Rome in AD 66, the long discontent of the Jews having been brought to a head and revolt by the cruelties of the procurators Albinus (AD 62–64) and Gessius Florus (AD 64–66).

Of the coins issued by the procurators those of Pontius Pilatus as procurator under Tiberius are of particular interest from his connection with the Crucifixion, and they are sought after by collectors for this reason. Their types are three ears of barley (**12**), or a simpulum or lituus (priestly emblems), and the name of Tiberius with his regnal year. Until the exact date of the Crucifixion is known, the actual coins struck in that year cannot be identified but, as the possible date might be AD 30,

12   Bronze coin of Pontius Pilatus, procurator AD 26–36. On the obverse, three ears of barley; on the reverse a simpulum and an inscription which ends giving the year of issue in Greek letters, LIS (= year 16 = AD 29/30).

13   One of the very rare Judaean silver shekels of year 4 of the First Revolt against Rome (AD 66–70); only a few specimens are known. The date is shown by the two letters above the chalice on the obverse; on the reverse is a branch with three buds (a lily?).

the coins inscribed with the sixteenth year of Tiberius would be those struck at that time.

When the Revolt of the Jews against Rome broke out in AD 66, the Jews commenced a coinage almost immediately and both silver and bronze coins were struck. The silver shekels (**13**), half, and quarter-shekels had obverse types of a cup or chalice and the inscription 'Shekel of Israel' (again in archaic Hebrew script). On the reverse is a branch with three buds (a lily?), which has been suggested as symbolic of Aaron's rod (Numbers 17:8), and an inscription 'Jerusalem the Holy'. The companion bronze pieces depict an amphora on the obverse and a vine-leaf on the reverse with the inscription 'Deliverance of Zion' (**14**). As the obverse inscription on the bronze coins, and as an additional feature on the silver, the year of the Revolt – 1 to 5 – is shown. A change was made in the bronze coins of year 4 (**15**). These were struck slightly larger in size and on the obverse is a bunch of twigs fastened together (*lulab*) with a citron (*ethrog*) on either side; these refer to the ceremonial connected with the feast of Tabernacles in Jewish ritual. A

14   Judaean bronze coin dated year 2 of the First Revolt with an amphora and a vine-leaf as its obverse and reverse types.

15   Bronze coin dated year 4 of the First Revolt. Here the types represent a *lulab* (bunch of twigs) flanked by an *ethrog* (citron), and a chalice on the reverse.

chalice appears on the reverse and the inscription 'For the Redemption of Zion'. The silver coins of years 4 and 5 are very rare and no bronze coins are known of year 5. After the revolt was crushed by the Romans in AD 70 special coins to celebrate this victory were struck by them in Palestine, and also in Rome (described below, p. 38).

To complete the details of the coins of the Jews, mention must be made of a further issue made at the time of the Second Revolt against Rome in AD 132–135 under Simon Barcochba ('Son of the star'), which may well account for the appearance of the star seen above the main type on some of his tetra-drachms. These coins depict on the obverse what has been variously described as the screen of the Temple with the Ark of the Covenant within, or the façade of a temple with the shrine in which the Scrolls of the Law were placed (**16**). Reifenberg (p. 36) gives references to the various opinions which have been expressed in the past on the interpretation of the type and,

16   Silver tetradrachm of the Second Revolt against Rome (AD 132–135) showing the façade of a temple on the obverse and the *lulab* and ethrog on the reverse.

following Cavedoni, he gives his own decision: 'We see on this coin the front of the Temple Bar-Kochba's followers intended to build' (following their hoped for liberation of Jerusalem) 'and into the interior of which a shrine containing the scrolls of the Law is put. . . . The horizonal lines inside the shrine indicate the shelves and the two points are meant to represent the scrolls of the Law'. He mentions also that the two points have been considered to represent the door-knobs.

As Herod's Temple – the second temple – had been destroyed by fire in AD 70, the last year of the First Revolt against Rome and some sixty years earlier than the Second Revolt, Reifenberg's interpretation appears to have very much to commend it. The shrine interpretation also, surely, accords more with the precepts of Jewish ritual. The Ark was in the Holy of Holies in the Temple and hidden behind the veil. Consequently, it was only visible to the High Priest on his solitary and annual entry into the Holy of Holies on the Day of Atonement. Hence, there is no reason why the Ark of the Covenant should be visible on the coin and a shrine would appear to be much more likely. A *lulab* and *ethrog* form the types of the reverse. The obverses are inscribed either 'Jerusalem' or 'Simon' and the reverses, 'The First (or Second) Year of the Redemption (or Freedom) of Israel'; in some cases the year is omitted. Smaller silver coins – denarii – were also struck and these have a wider range of types, as do the companion bronze coins. The types include a vase, lyre, bunches of grapes (**17**), palm branch, or trumpets, and some carry the name of 'Eleazar the Priest', and others 'First Year of the Redemption of Israel' as the inscription, or 'For the Freedom of Jerusalem'.

17   Bronze coin of the Second Revolt with a palm tree and a bunch of grapes as its types.

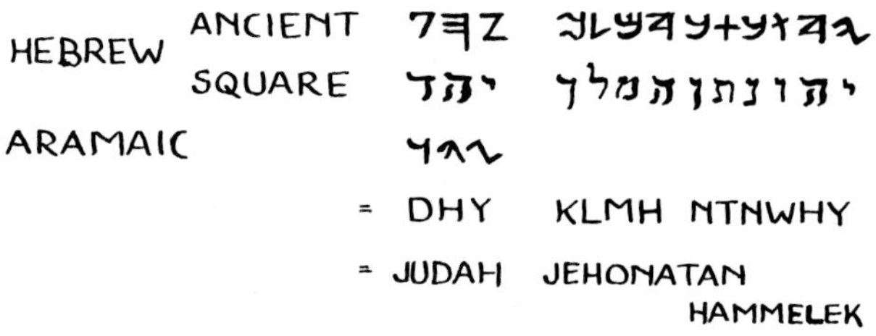

HEBREW	ANCIENT	𐤆𐤉𐤃	𐤂𐤁𐤉𐤅𐤕𐤍𐤕𐤉𐤄𐤔𐤋𐤌
	SQUARE	יהד	יהונתנהמלך
ARAMAIC		�	

= DHY   KLMH NTNWHY

= JUDAH   JEHONATAN
                    HAMMELEK

(THE SCRIPTS ARE READ FROM RIGHT TO LEFT: Y=J)

A strange feature of the Jewish coinage is that, with the exception of the names of some rulers which appeared in Greek characters, from the earliest to the latest issues the inscriptions are always shown in archaic Hebrew script, this having long been superseded by the square script. The square Hebrew had itself been replaced for all normal purposes by Aramaic, a language of the Persian empire, the square characters being employed only for religious purposes. Presumably it was simply ultra conservatism that decreed the use of the archaic and obsolete script on the coins. Aramaic was the language spoken by the people at the time and few ordinary folk could read Hebrew, but from Luke 4:16–17 it is evident that Jesus, although He would have actually spoken mostly in Aramaic, was able to read the square Hebrew in which the scriptures were written.

Before passing on to the next chapter it will be well to summarise the state of the coinage in Palestine during the lifetime of Jesus. From the foregoing it will be seen that there was no single coinage throughout the land as is customary at the present time in most countries of the world. There were in circulation many different coins which would include the silver, bronze, and possibly a few gold pieces, issued by the various Greek cities of the land and of nearby countries, and these might well include some coins struck many years earlier. Also still in circulation would be the bronze coins of the Jewish series struck before 37 BC, and the issues of the Herodian kings and the Roman procurators which followed the Jewish series. The coins of Rome itself would also be known and used, these being in gold, silver, and 'brass', the latter an unscientific name by which some Roman base metal coins are frequently known to collectors. With all these different coinages circulating side by side, and as they were not necessarily adjusted one to another and struck on the same weight standards, the need for the money changers is fully evident (Mark 11:15 and John 2:15). This necessity is made even more apparent when it is realised that some of the many and varied coinages could only be used for specified purposes, such as the use of Roman coin for payment of the Roman taxes.

2

THE COINS OF THE BIBLE

It is hoped that the preceding brief sketch of the world's coinages down to New Testament times will have been sufficient to outline a vast subject and thus to provide a background for a consideration of some of the references to money and particularly to coins, as they are to be found mentioned in the Bible.

As the invention of coinage took place at the end of, or soon after, the reign of Manasseh, king of Judah, *c.* 697–641 BC (2 Chronicles 33:1) and therefore about the time of the prophet Jeremiah, reference to gold and silver earlier than this must, of necessity, refer to the metals and their employment as bullion and not as coin.

In the earliest times people were largely agricultural workers and the exchange of goods was conducted purely and simply by barter – the exchange of one article for another of equal or agreed value. Later, in certain parts, oxen and sheep became used as a type of currency to facilitate this exchange and amongst certain peoples the use of this cattle currency remained for many years. The English words 'fee' and 'pecuniary' are amongst a number to be found in various languages which spring from roots in ancient tongues which mean cattle (Anglo-Saxon, *feoh*; Latin, *pecus*). After metals came to be used, valued, and weighed, it became customary to equate certain agreed weights of metal as the price of an ox, and thus a metallic currency came into existence. These equivalent weights of metal varied according to the intrinsic value of the metal itself, as in gold, which was accounted to be of the greatest value, the most usual standard was about 131 grains of gold as equal to the ox, with copper some 3000 times as much, but variations according to district and development are also to be found. The units of metal equated to the ox were known to the Greeks as talents – the Greek word Ταλάντον meaning a scale, or a weight placed on a scale – and to the Babylonians as shekels. These names at that time were significant of measures of weight, but the word shekel later was used as the name of the Jewish coin. Quotations which illustrate the use of the word as a measure of weight include 'the weight of whose spear weighed three hundred shekels of brass in weight' (2 Samuel 21:16); 'So David gave to Ornan for the place six hundred shekels of gold by weight' (1 Chronicles 21:25); and 'thy meat which thou shalt eat shall be by weight, twenty shekels a day' (Ezekiel 4:10).

During the Mosaic period the shekel was reckoned as the fiftieth part of the manah or mina (which is translated as a pound in 1 Kings 10:17 and Luke 19:13), and the mina the sixtieth part of the talent to which reference is found in Exodus 25:39. Later, in the Regal period, this same 'light' Babylonic shekel of about 131 grains was known as the 'shekel of the sanctuary' (Exodus 30:13), and it remained in use for the weighing of gold and was then the one hundredth part of the mina. Proof of this can be found in 1 Kings 10:17, 'three pounds of gold' and in 2 Chronicles 9:16, 'three hundred shekels of gold' as these are both references to the same incident. For the weighing of silver and bronze, a new shekel of twice the weight (about 262 grains) was introduced, and this 'heavy' shekel was in all probability known as the 'king's shekel' (2 Samuel 14:26). Following the return from the captivity in Babylon, the 'light' shekel was still used for gold, but the Phoenician standard of about 220 grains to the shekel was employed for silver and it was at about this weight that the

Jewish silver coins of the First Revolt against the Romans (AD 66–70) were struck.

From the currency aspect, however, a reference in Genesis 23:16 is of prime importance, as it is stated in connection with the purchase of the cave of Machpelah, 'Abraham weighed to Ephron . . . four hundred shekels of silver, current money with the merchant' and this makes it clear that at every transaction it was necessary to weigh out the required amount of metal with the balance (**18**), this process being mentioned also in Jeremiah 32:10, '. . . and weighed him the money in the balances'. From finds of actual specimens there is evidence that a metallic currency in the form of small wedges, pellets, or rings of standard weight was in later times employed in the course of trade, and these objects might well have been

18 Wall painting in the tomb of Benia, called Pahekem, at Thebes (modern Luxor) showing the owner supervising the weighing of gold and electrum (a natural alloy of gold and silver) rings whilst scribes note down the amounts. Fourteenth century BC.

reckoned by tale: in other words, counted out as is customary with modern coins. References to the passing of metal by tale can be found in the Bible in Genesis 20:16 and 33:19, and to a wedge of gold in Joshua 7:21.

The trouble caused by the necessity of weighing out the metal for most business transactions of the time must well have given added point to the desirability of introducing a medium which obviated the use of this lengthy process, as it would be much quicker to count out the required number of pieces than to weigh out the metal. A coinage therefore answers this requirement to the best advantage. It would be a great step forward from the earlier currency wedges, pellets, or rings, as the coins which are easily portable and handled are, in addition, marked by the issuing authority in some manner to signify their good weight and metal. It will be remembered that a coin is defined as a piece of metal of intrinsic or token value, weighed out to an agreed weight standard, and marked as a guarantee of both metal and weight, as was mentioned in Chapter 1. Some writers have suggested the 300 drachms of gold mentioned by Ezra were Persian darics and therefore that this is the first mention of actual coins in the Bible. If they were coins they could not have been darics as they were not introduced until about 510 BC, which is some twenty-eight years after the return from the Exile. It is possible that they could have been the gold coins struck by the Persians following the types of the Lydian king, Croesus, but this appears to be unlikely and it seems more probable that in this instance the word drachm was employed as a unit of weight.

Passing on to the New Testament, a fair degree of certainty can be reached when consideration is given to the three major references to coins which occur as part of the actual narrative of the Gospels. The main difficulty encountered when dealing with the coin references in the parables is that there is no certainty whether the writers of the Gospels may have substituted the names of coins current at the actual time of writing (mid-first century AD onwards) rather than by recording the names of the coins in actual use in Palestine during the life of Jesus.

Possibly the most frequently quoted reference to a coin is found in Matthew 22:19 (Mark 12:15, and Luke 20:24), where it is recorded that Jesus asked for a specimen of the tribute money to be brought to Him before giving His answer to the question 'Is it lawful to give tribute unto Caesar?' This annual tribute, or tax, of a denarius was imposed upon Judaea when it was reduced to a Roman province in AD 6. It had to be paid by all males between the ages of 14 and 65 and all females between the ages of 12 and 65; as a Roman tax, it would have to be paid in Roman coins – silver denarii (**19,20**).

The translation of the word δηνάριον in the Authorised Version of the Bible as a penny is most unfortunate as it gives an entirely incorrect impression of the value in the purchasing power of the coin when considered side by side with the British penny of recent times. Prior to the change to decimal coinage in Great Britain, the *d.* of the symbols £.*s.d.* represented the *denarius*, and the British penny was derived in the first instance from the Roman denarius, but many changes took place in the centuries between which have made the modern penny very different from the Roman prototype. The currency value of the denarius was far in excess of the British penny: it was a suitable and agreeable payment for a day's labour in the vineyard, as will be found in Matthew 20:1ff., although it has been suggested this may represent a generous amount. Two denarii were suitable payment to the innkeeper by the good Samaritan (Luke 10:35) for looking after the needs of the man who fell among thieves – two modern pence would hardly be sufficient! Altogether, the more modern translation of the denarius as a 'silver piece' is far less likely to provide an incorrect understanding of the coin in the mind of the reader.

During the Roman Republic a wide variety of types had appeared on successive issues of denarii, but from early in the reign of Augustus his portrait became the standard type for the obverse of his denarii and aurei. This same precedent was continued by Tiberius after he succeeded to the throne on the death of Augustus in AD 14, and as he reigned until AD 37 he was the emperor during the ministry of Jesus. It is therefore to be expected that one of his denarii would have been handed to

Jesus. Even this fact, however, is open to debate. It can only be certain the coin in question was a denarius but, of which issue?

If the current coins in a purse are examined at any time, it would be most unusual if they were all of one date, even though they could well be of one denomination; some might be of quite recent mintage but others might have been struck many years earlier. Such would be the case at the time of the incident under consideration and the question to which an answer is required is, which denarius would be most likely to have been in common use in Palestine at the time? Augustus struck a number of denarii at eastern mints, probably Ephesus and Pergamum, between 30 and possibly 15 BC and it is possible that a few could still be in circulation in Palestine. However, from 2 BC to the end of the reign, the great majority of the denarii were probably struck at the Imperial mint at Lugdunum (Lyons in France) and were of one reverse type depicting Gaius and Lucius (grandsons of Augustus) each holding a spear and shield; priestly implements are seen between them (**19**). The inscription on these coins reads C.L. CAESARES. AVGVSTI. F. COS. DESIG. PRINC. IVVENT ('Caius and Lucius, the two Caesars, sons of Augustus, elected consuls, princes of youth').

In AD 15 a few denarii appeared depicting Tiberius in a four-horse-chariot but, as the coins depicting the two Caesars had been in use over a period of several years, they would have been far more numerous and widely spread. On issuing denarii of his own after becoming emperor, Tiberius continued the precedent established by Augustus, and virtually the only type used in his reign is that which depicts a seated female

19   Silver denarius of Augustus (27 BC–AD 14) with his name and titles (his image and superscription) and, on the reverse, the young Caius and Lucius Caesars, his heirs.

20 Silver denarius of Tiberius (AD 14–37) with the emperor's portrait and a seated figure on the reverse which may be his mother Livia or a personification of Pax (Peace).

figure (**20**). This figure is probably Livia, the wife of Augustus and mother of Tiberius, but it is thought by some numismatists to be a personification of Pax (Peace). On the obverse is the customary portrait, now of Tiberius as emperor, and around which is the inscription TI. CAESAR. DIVI. AVG. F. AVGVSTVS, the inscription being completed by the words PONTIF. MAXIM. on either side of the figure on the reverse ('Tiberius, Caesar Augustus, Son of the Divine Augustus – High Priest'). This gives the point to the words 'image and superscription' (Matthew 22:20).

From time to time numismatists have suggested other coins to have been the type of the coin handed to Jesus, but from the name of the coin denomination in the original Greek text – δηνάριον – some of these suggestions must be considered as invalid, and the date of mintage – *after* the life of Jesus – rules out others. As the incident took place perhaps about AD 28, Tiberius had been emperor some 15 or 16 years so there would have been plenty of time for his coins to have circulated throughout the Roman world and they were certainly used in Palestine. Against this, finds of coin hoards in Palestine suggest that the denarii of Augustus enjoyed a far greater circulation and finds are more numerous. For example, a hoard of some 4,500 silver coins found on Mount Carmel in 1960 and buried after AD 54 consisted mainly of shekels and half-shekels of Tyre, but it also contained 160 denarii of Augustus and Tiberius, nearly all of which were the two Caesars type coins of Augustus. It has long been held that a denarius of Tiberius was the coin actually handed to Jesus and, accordingly, they are commonly known as 'Tribute Pennies', but on numismatic grounds, a denarius of Augustus of the C. L. Caesares type is much more likely to have been the coin of the incident. It would appear, therefore, that no concrete proof can be given or expected, but either issue would fit the context well as both carry the 'image and superscription' of 'Caesar'. In the New Testament other references to denarii are to be found in Mark 14:5 and the Revelation of John 6:6.

From early times under Jewish law every male person had to pay an annual tribute or due towards the support of the Temple (Exodus, 30:13), the 'Temple Tribute' being of the value of a didrachm (two drachms) or the equivalent of it, a half-shekel. When, as recorded in Matthew 17:24, Peter was asked if his master paid the tribute money, the word employed in the Greek text is δίδραχμα – a didrachm. The translation of the New Testament by Weymouth reads more closely to the original than some other translations, verse 24 being given by him as 'After their arrival at Capernaum the collectors of the half-shekel came and asked Peter, "Does not your Teacher pay the half-shekel?"' Accordingly, the coin found in the mouth of the fish (verse 27) must have been of the weight of a shekel (it is called here a stater or standard coin – στατηρα) as it is mentioned that it was of sufficient value to pay the tribute for two people. There is every probability that the actual coin found would have been a shekel of Tyre (**23**), to which coins reference will again be made later. They were not only struck in large numbers over a long period and would have been circulating freely in the district but they were actually specified in Jewish law for use in the payment of the tribute.

The third specific reference to coins in the Gospel narratives to be considered is that of the 'thirty pieces of silver' which were accepted by Judas Iscariot for the betrayal (Matthew 26:15). The identification of the actual coins employed has presented considerable difficulty to numismatists in the past and views on the problem held for many years have now had to be abandoned in the light of fresh discoveries and modern theories. In a number of religious foundations on the Continent coins have been treasured that were supposedly specimens of the actual 'thirty pieces'. A number of these have been found

21 Silver didrachm of Rhodes, *c.* 304–109 BC, having the same types as the tetradrachms, a radiate head of Helios on the obverse and a full rose on the reverse.

to be tetradrachms struck in the island of Rhodes three or four centuries before the life of Christ. Their obverse type shows a facing head of the sun-god Helios surrounded by rays of light and this has been mistaken for a representation of the head of Christ wearing the crown of thorns (**21**). The reverse type, a rose, has also been thought to have been the rose of Sharon, symbolical of the Resurrection, whereas it is actually the emblem of Helios and a punning allusion to the name of the mint. These 'Judas Pennies' as they have sometimes been called, would hardly have been current in quantity in Palestine so long after having been struck, although an odd piece or two might still have been found on the tables of the money changers. Their use as the 'thirty pieces' can therefore be ruled out, as can also the Christian connotation which has been applied to the types.

The Jewish shekels of the First Revolt against Rome (**13**) were, for many years, considered to have been struck as the first Jewish coins of 138 BC, and have also been identified as the coins handed to Judas. Just as cast copies of the 'Judas Pennies' are known, multitudes of copies of the First Revolt shekels have been made, in some cases for fraudulent purposes maybe, but mainly to provide followers of Christ with easily obtained relics of the betrayal (**22**). Appearing first in the middle of the sixteenth century, the vast majority of these copies have only a superficial resemblance to the original shekels, most of them being greater in diameter and much thinner; these and other differences can easily be seen by anyone on comparison with a genuine coin. Until quite recently it was possible to purchase these reproductions and many were sold accompanied by

22   A false shekel which has only a passing likeness to the genuine shekels (see no. 13 above).

printed descriptions such as the following:

> Fac-similes of the JERUSALEM SHEKEL, the Coin for which our SAVIOUR JESUS CHRIST was Sold.
>
> Taken from a genuine Coin, which is generally ascribed to Simon Maccabaus, who reigned King of Israel 172–142; it was issued in the second year of his reign, consequently 2023 years ago. See 1 Macabees, chap. XIII, verse 41; the 171st year spoken of in verse 51.
>
> Explanation of the Coinage – Verso: Jerusalem Shekel year 2. Recto: Liberator of Israel.

There are errors in this description. The dates of Simon Maccabaeus' rule as High Priest and Prince are 142–135 BC, and the error regarding the mention of the 171st year was caused probably by reference to the 171st year of the Seleucid era (which commenced in 312 BC) and which would be 142–141 BC. Also, the translations of the Hebrew inscriptions are 'Shekel of Israel' and 'Jerusalem the Holy'. The suggestion that these shekels were in fact the coins of the 'thirty pieces' has now been ruled out as impossible by overwhelming evidence of style and epigraphical detail amongst other points, including hoard finds, which date them firmly to the First Revolt of the Jews against Rome (AD 66–70), some 35 years or so after the Crucifixion.

It is possible that Roman denarii might have been the coins given as the 'thirty pieces', but it is far more probable that coins of greater value would have been employed for the purpose.

23 Silver shekel of Tyre with the head of Melkart (Herakles) and, on the reverse, an eagle standing. Coins with these types were struck between *c.* 126 BC and AD 65; here the date appears to the left of the eagle: EK = year 25 = 102/101 BC.

As the temple treasury would be filled with many Tyrian shekels and half-shekels paid as temple tribute, these coins seem to be the most likely to have been given to Judas for the betrayal and subsequently returned by him to the chief priests (**23**). If this is the case, the sum of money might approximate to something like £4 to £5 of English money before inflation, but again, this is hardly a fair comparison as the purchasing power would have been far greater than the amount of the present day: a better understanding can be gained if the 'thirty pieces' are approximated in value to something like fair wages (Matthew 20:1ff.) for 120 days labour. As the Greek text gives simply τριάκοντα 'αργύρια – thirty pieces of silver – nothing more definite can be suggested, but the Tyrian shekels would seem to be by far the most probable coins employed for this payment.

Turning now to the parables of Jesus we find a number of different coins mentioned. However, as was pointed out earlier in this chapter, references to them are complicated by the fact that the authors of the Gospels may well have substituted the names of coins in everyday use at the time of writing. Such names would be well known to their readers, both as actual coins and as to their purchasing power, but they might also have been the contemporary names of coins rather than those mentioned by Jesus actually at the time when the parables were spoken. Even so, the names of the various coins as they appear in the Greek text can be considered.

The denarius has already been mentioned as the coin of the tribute money and also in the parables of the Good Samaritan and the labourers in the vineyard, where they were considered as a fair day's wages. Other mentions of the coins are to be found in Matthew 18:28 and Luke 7:41. In the parable of the lost piece of silver (Luke 15:8), the coin is given in the text as a δραχμὰ, the silver drachm or drachma of the Greek coin series which was roughly equivalent in size and weight to the Roman denarius.

At this point mention should again be made of the mina (μνᾶ) which is translated in Luke 19:13 as a pound, although it was a unit of weight and not a coin denomination. The same applies to the talents of Matthew 18:24 and 25:15. The relationship in value between the mina and the actual coins varied at different mints, being considered as containing between 100 and 60 drachms according to the weight standard employed for the coins of the particular locality. As the drachm was somewhat similar to the denarius, the mina represented a sizeable amount of currency. The talents were therefore of very considerable currency value since the mina itself was the sixtieth part of the talent.

When considering the references to bronze coins in the parables, much greater difficulty is experienced in linking the denominations named to actual coins. Several are named in the Gospels – chalkus, lepton, assarion, quadrans – but there is little definite knowledge of how these different denominations were adjusted to one another, or to the silver coinage, if at all. There is reason to believe that in Attica eight chalkoi were equal to a silver obol and that seven lepta equalled the chalkus, but in other parts it appears that twelve chalkoi were equal to the obol. Further, there is little evidence of the actual coins to which these various names were applied (at least those in the Greek series) as it is only in a very few instances that the name of the denomination is stated on the coin. For this reason numismatists normally refer to Greek bronze coins by their diameter in millimetres, as was mentioned in Chapter 1.

Probably the most quoted and well known reference to bronze coins is that of the widow's mites – the lepta of Mark

THE COINS OF THE BIBLE 35

24 Common first century BC Judaean light-weight bronze copies of the prutoth of Alexander Jannaeus (no. 8 above); frequently known as 'widow's mites'.

12:42, and Luke 21:2. It seems reasonably certain that the original reference to the 'two mites' in the parable would have been to prutoth or half-prutoth of the Jewish high priests struck before 37 BC, or to the coins of the early Roman procurators, and accordingly these Jewish coins are sometimes referred to as 'mites' (**24**). By calling them lepta in his text, Mark added emphasis to the small size of the widow's contribution to the treasury as apparently the lepta were the smallest Greek coins (the word lepton meaning 'the thin one'), the very size and insignificance of them being a very apt comparison with the larger coins cast into the treasury by the rich from their plenty. For further emphasis to his readers Mark adds also λεπτὰ δύο, ὅ ἐστιν κοδράντης ('two mites which make a farthing') Here he equates the two lepta as equal to a quadrans (**25**), the smallest coin of the Roman series, four of which were equal to the *as*. There is no knowledge of whether the Greek and Roman coins were in any way adjusted to one another (if at all), but undoubtedly Mark was anxious to present all understandable possible detail to his readers to stress the message of the parable. The lepton is also named in Luke 12:59 and is there translated as a mite, but in the parallel passage in Matthew 5:26, the coin named is the quadrans, which again is translated as a farthing.

25 Bronze quadrans of Augustus struck in 5 BC. It has the names of the monetary magistrates around an altar with a bowl-shaped top.

The chalkus (χαλκοῦζ) was certainly a bronze denomination in certain parts of the Greek world, but the word χαλκὸν was used also to represent bronze coins generally, as 'coppers' is now used in English to indicate two pence and pence collectively. It is this sense that applies to χαλκὸν in the reference made in Matthew 10:9 which is translated as 'Provide neither gold, nor silver, nor brass in your purses'. The word brass, for χαλκὸν, in the translation appears in Tyndale's Bible of 1526, and it was used to represent money even before that time.

In Matthew 10:29, a further coin denomination is named – the assarion, ἀσσαρίον (Luke 12:6, ἀσσαρίων) which is again translated as a farthing, or as a penny in some texts. There is an example of a Greek coin struck at Chios during the first century or so of the Christian era, which is actually named an assarion and which gives in this instance an idea of its size and weight. In view of the extensive variations in weight to be found in the Greek bronze issues, no reliance can be placed upon all coins of similar weight being known by this name. However, the assarion would certainly be a higher denomination than the quadrans and lepton.

To conclude this survey the point should be stressed once again that although the references to bronze coins are appropriate in their respective contexts by indicating the meanings and interpretations of the parables as actually spoken by Jesus, in most cases the parable references cannot be related to any particular coin or issue. In the contexts such relationships to actual coins were unnecessary and, in general, the names of the coin denominations as recorded by the writers of the Gospels appear to be in the nature of indications of approximate values – probably in contemporary terminology – rather than direct and exact references to any particular coin or issue which would be unfamiliar to their readers.

3

THE MILVIAN BRIDGE
AND AFTER

To appreciate the significance and the effects of the conversion of Constantine the Great to Christianity with the far reaching changes it brought to the Roman empire and to its coinage, the earlier background to this event should first be considered.

From the time of Augustus, the first emperor of Rome (27 BC–AD 14) the pattern of the coinage he laid down remained for many years. Apart from the Greek Imperial issues already mentioned, what might be termed more or less a single coinage throughout the empire was normally used, although it was struck at times at mints other than Rome itself. A portrait of the emperor was the normal type on the obverse and therefore coins are easily obtainable which show the portraits of the emperors during New Testament times – Augustus (Luke 2:1), at the time of the Nativity (**19**); Tiberius (Luke 3:1) at the Crucifixion (**20**); Caligula; Claudius, to whom reference is made in Acts 11:28; and Nero (Acts 25:12) to whom St Paul appealed and under whom he and St Peter suffered martyrdom probably in AD 64 during the terrible persecutions of the Christians (**1**). The types of the reverses of the coins vary to a very great extent. The Roman gods and goddesses, personifications, animals, and buildings are all to be found, but what are probably the most interesting of all the many types are the coins which make special references to contemporary events in the life of the emperor and people, as the Romans employed many of their coins to convey news and propaganda to the people using them. A good example of this is provided by the series of coins struck by Vespasian and Titus to commemorate and advertise their victories over the Jews when the First Revolt of AD 66–70 was subdued, and obviously they make reference to the events from the Roman standpoint. These celebrated coins are of slightly varied type but basically they depict a palm tree beside which is shown a Jew and a Jewess, or female personification of Judaea, in an attitude of sadness and subjection, together with the inscription IVDAEA, or IVDAEA CAPTA, which, with the type, implies 'the overwhelming defeat of Judaea' (**26**). On a few pieces the emperor himself is depicted and the implication provided by the types and inscription would clearly be evident to the Roman citizens using the coins. At this same time, a tax was imposed upon the Jews – the Fiscus Iudaicus – by Vespasian, this being a continuation of the Jewish 'Temple tribute' of one didrachm, but now diverted to the worship of Jupiter Capitolinus. Nerva, who was emperor of Rome from 96 to 98, to some extent eased

26   Orichalcum sestertius of Vespasian (AD 69–79) celebrating the capture of Judaea on its reverse type showing the emperor and a subjugated Jewess beside a plam tree.

the rigorous methods of collecting this tax employed by his predecessors and he announced this fact on some of his sester-tii, thus providing a further example of the use of a coin type for propaganda.

The Christians were subjected to further persecution during the reign of Trajan Decius (249–251) and some form of propaganda motif may well have been in the minds of the authorities when a series of his coins was struck which show on the reverses portraits of a number of the earlier emperors who had been consecrated after their death. The consecration and deification of an emperor who had met with the approval of the people formed a vital part of the Roman religion which held the worship of the emperor as an essential feature. This series of coins would, therefore, bring back the thoughts of the users to the established religion at a time when Christianity was beginning to make itself a power with which to be reckoned, as it was vitally opposed to the Roman religious policy.

During the persecutions the Christians were denied the use of their places of worship and cemeteries, but in 261 the emperor Gallienus gave official permission to use them once again. This reign also provides what may be the first direct Christian reference on a coin, as a piece struck at Mediolanum (Milan) with the name and portrait of Salonina, the wife of Gallienus, has for the reverse type a seated figure of the empress around which is the inscription AVG IN PACE ('The Empress in peace'). Salonina was reputed to have been a Christian, but whether this inscription (27), which has a distinctly Christian sound, has any such connection remains a debatable point, and strong arguments can be put forward from both sides.

Early in the fourth century AD bitter persecutions took place once again. The empire was by then divided into two parts with Diocletian as Augustus or emperor of the eastern half and with Galerius under him as his Caesar; Maximian and Con-stantius Chlorus held similar positions in the western half.

27 Possibly the first direct Christian reference on a coin of the Empress Salonina, wife of Gallienus (AD 253–268), AVG IN PACE ('The Empress in Peace').

Galerius was the chief instigator of these renewed persecutions, but at first Diocletian did not participate. Diocletian's wife, Prisca, and his daughter, Valeria, are believed to have been Christians, and many others were holding positions of trust and responsibility in his service, but eventually in 303 he capitulated and agreed to the policy of his Caesar. In 305 Diocletian abdicated and Galerius became Augustus in his place; in 311, just before his death, Galerius brought the persecutions to an end, although they did occur occasionally in the East until 324.

The persecutions were mainly in the eastern half of the empire and Constantius Chlorus, Caesar in the West, although not a Christian, may well have had considerable sympathy with the faith. His first wife, Helena, is reputed to have discovered at Jerusalem the sepulchre and the wood of the True Cross of Christ. Their son Constantine (known later as Constantine the Great) became Caesar in 306 on the death of his father and Augustus in 308. Constantine became the sole emperor of both halves of the empire on the defeat of Licinius in 324. There is little doubt that Constantine was strongly influenced by the teachings of the Christians even before his actual conversion, and therefore his adoption of Christianity may not have been so reactionary as has at times been suggested. During the third century the Roman religion was itself showing signs of change from the polytheism of the earlier times to something of a monotheistic conception with Sol Invictus (the Sun-God) as the principle deity. This was just another step towards the eventual adoption of Christianity as the religion of the State, which, broadly speaking, required

then only the change of the Supreme Being. Such was the state
of things when the vision appeared to Constantine; an occur-
rence which was to him so full of meaning that in obedience to
it he went into battle in the name of Christ on 27 October 312
against Maxentius, and was victorious over him at the Milvian
Bridge (cover illustration).

Eusebius and Lactantius are the two ancient authorities who
have recorded accounts of the visions of Constantine which
must have had an exceptional effect upon him; some modern
scholars, however, have cast considerable doubt upon them.
Eusebius, who became Bishop of Caesarea about the year 311,
records that Constantine prayed with fervent entreaty for help
in his present difficulties and that in answer to his prayer he saw
in the sky above the setting sun, a vision of a cross of light and
an inscription HOC SIGNO VICTOR ERIS ('Under this sign you will
be victorious'). Then, in his sleep that night Christ appeared to
him commanding him to make a likeness of the Cross and to
use it as a safeguard in all engagements with his enemies. A
second experience occurred whilst Constantine was encamped
in the neighbourhood of the Milvian Bridge. It is described by
Lactantius who became tutor to Constantine's eldest son,
Crispus, and he recounts that Constantine was directed in a
dream to make the sign of Christ upon the shields of his
soldiers and thus to join battle. This sign is the Chi-Rho, a
monogram composed of the first letters of the name of Christ
in Greek, Χριστός.

Considerable discussion has taken place concerning these
visions but, whether it is felt they are to be relied upon as fact or
not, something exceptional must have influenced Constantine.
He was not only victorious over Maxentius at the battle of the
Milvian Bridge; but in 313, by the Edict of Milan, universal
toleration of Christianity was proclaimed. Persecutions occasionally took place in the East until Constantine's defeat of his
earlier colleague Licinius in 324, and Christianity then became
officially commended and the established custom of emperor
worship was forbidden. Undoubtedly Constantine had given
peace to the Church. Christianity eventually became the
State religion and, although it may not have been immediately,

Constantine himself embraced the faith and he was baptised on his death-bed in 337.

In obedience to the vision, Constantine had the Chi-Rho engraved upon his helmet and also had it painted upon the shields of his soldiers although it is highly probable that at the time they would hardly appreciate what it meant or for what it stood. Similarly, a jewelled banner (the labarum) emblazoned with the Chi-Rho was made and carried before Constantine's army into battle. Numismatic evidence of this can be found as, on some coins, the Chi-Rho is seen actually engraved on the helmet worn by Constantine. The coins which show this feature have as their reverse type two female winged figures (personifications of victory) holding a shield, and the inscription reads VICTORIAE LAETAE PRINC. PERP. ('To the glorious victory of our eternal Emperor'). These small bronze pieces are quite common as they were struck in large quantities at several different mints. Most of them show the helmeted head of Constantine on the obverse, but those on which the helmet is shown embellished with the Chi-Rho are very rare and were struck at Siscia (Sisak) in 319 (**28**).

28   Rare bronze coin of Constantine I (AD 308–337) struck at the mint of Siscia and showing the emperor with the Chi-Rho monogram on his helmet.

Apart from the gold solidi which were the Constantinian counterparts of the aurei of the early empire, the small bronze pieces similar to those just mentioned were almost the only coins struck at the time. Many different types were employed on both gold and bronze, and on one very common type of bronze which shows two soldiers holding shields and spears, with the inscription GLORIA EXERCITVS ('The glory of the army'), the Chi-Rho is found at times emblazoned on a banner between the soldiers or as a symbol in the field (the numismatic term for the space on the coin not actually occupied by the type). Such symbols and monograms appear frequently on ancient coins and are often employed to indicate issues, mints, the monetary magistrates responsible for the coins, or for other purposes of control. A similar monogram to that now under discussion had appeared many years earlier on some bronze Ptolemaic coins struck at Alexandria, but at that time obviously there was no question of it being significant of the name of Christ: it would, in all probability, stand for the name of the monetary magistrate responsible for the particular issue. There is no doubt, however, about the correctness of the meaning at the time of Constantine as proof is supplied by complementary types which appear frequently throughout the years that follow. One such coin of Constantine (**29**) depicts the labarum standing upon a serpent, and with the serpent symbolising the powers of evil, the meaning of the type is made apparent by the inscription SPES PVBLICA ('The Hope of the people').

29   Reverse type of a bronze coin of Constantine I, the Great, showing a labarum (standard) surmounted by the Chi-Rho monogram. Struck at Constantinopolis, AD 327–328.

After Constantine had obtained full sovereignty over the whole empire following the defeat of his former colleague Licinius in 324, he set about rebuilding the old Greek city of Byzantium (the forerunner of Istanbul on the Bosphorus) as his new capital, and this he dedicated on 17 May 330 under the name of Constantinopolis. This was to be the Christian capital of the empire and to which the seat of government was partly transferred from Rome; thus the empire virtually became divided into two separate parts which grew wider apart as the years passed.

Following the death of Constantine, memorial coins were struck. Constantine is shown consecrated, but there is little doubt that this had a very different significance from that implied by the consecration of the earlier pagan emperors. On one coin Constantine is shown standing with the letters VN MR on either side; these being abbreviations for VENERANDA MEMORIA ('In revered memory'). On a second type the emperor is shown in a chariot drawn by four horses above which is seen the hand of God (**30**). In the minds of the designers of this type there might well have been some such idea as the ascent of Elijah (2 Kings 2:11) and it provides the first instance of the symbolic representation of God himself whose hand was to appear again in Roman and later series, either by itself or crowning the emperor.

30   Reverse of a bronze memorial coin for Constantine the Great showing the emperor in a four-horse chariot above which is the Hand of God. Struck at the mint on Cyzicus on the southern shore of the Sea of Marmara, AD 337–339.

As the old paganism gradually gave way to Christianity – there was no sudden and dramatic change of official religious policy, and there was even a brief return to paganism under Julian the Apostate – so the old gods gradually disappear from the coin types. Victory remains a popular type and the use of this pagan representation in both Christian and secular context must appear rather strange. It may well be that by this time she had taken to herself some semi-Christian meaning as the Angel of Victory.

During the reign of the sons of Constantine a frequently used type is a representation of the emperor holding either one or two labarums, and the Chi-Rho symbol appears freely (**31**). A further big step was taken between September 352 and August 353 when the usurper Magnentius and Decentius, his

31   Reverse of a bronze coin of Constantius II (AD 337–361) showing the emperor holding two labarums, each inscribed with the Chi-Rho monogram. Struck at the mint of Siscia, AD 350.

brother and Caesar, issued coins from the Gallic mints under their control – Ambianum (Amiens); Treveri (Trier); Lugdunum (Lyons); and Arelate (Arles) – which show the sacred monogram as the main and only type of the reverse (**32**). This can only be a very definite Christian type and the symbolism is completed by the addition of the letters alpha and omega, the first and last letters of the Greek alphabet. The full significance of the whole, therefore, is a direct allusion to Revelation 21:6: 'I am the Alpha and Omega; the beginning and the end'. This type also appears on some coins struck at the mint of Treveri in the name of Constantius II, the legitimate emperor, during the revolt against Magnentius in 353. Vetranio, who also usurped the throne in 350 for some ten months, and Constantius II (Caesar 323–337; Augustus 337–361), both strike with the wording of the vision of Constantine the Great HOC SIGNO VICTOR ERIS, and which, therefore, would appear to give corroboration of the correctness of this wording rather than IN HOC SIGNO VINCES, the alternative, which is found on the coins of Portugal struck during the last few centuries.

32   The Chi-Rho monogram between A and ω (alpha and omega) on the reverse of a bronze coin of Magnentius struck at Lugdunum (Lyons), AD 352–353.

An entirely new departure is found on the coins of Aelia Flaccilla, wife of Theodosius the Great (379–395), as a reverse type of hers shows the female personification of Victory inscribing the Chi-Rho on a shield with the inscription SALVS REIPVBLICAE ('The safety, or salvation, of the State'). This type (**33**) seems to hark back to Constantine's monogram painted on the shields of his soldiers in obedience to the Heavenly vision, and it may well have been suggested by it. As the years pass, this type makes several appearances but it seems only to have been employed by the empresses and only on the gold coins, apart from the bronze coins of Aelia Flaccilla herself.

33   Victory inscribing the Chi-Rho on a shield on the reverse of a bronze coin of the Empress Aelia Flacilla. Struck at Constantinopole, AD 383–388.

As the Roman empire in the West draws to its close the emperor, or Victory holding a long cross, frequently appear as coin types and the orb surmounted by a cross is introduced. A completely new departure is to be found on a gold solidus of Marcian, emperor in the East, who struck a coin with a special type in celebration of his marriage to Pulcheria in 450. On the reverse of this very rare coin Marcian and Pulcheria are seen joining hands, and the figure of Christ himself is shown standing between them (**34**). All three figures are shown nimbate, but the nimbus of Christ is surmounted by a cross. The hand of God had appeared on the memorial coins of Constantine the Great as part of a coin type (**30**), but this is the first of a numbr of varied representations of Christ himself to appear. The culmination of Christian types in the Roman series is reached during the three-month reign of Olybrius in 472,

34 Gold solidus, struck at Constantinopolis, of Marcian (AD 450–457) showing Christ standing between the emperor and the empress, Pulcheria.

when a solidus (**35**) was struck on which the cross is surrounded by an inscription which is obviously Christian – SALVS MVNDI ('The Salvation of the World'). The significance of this needs no further comment.

Romulus Augustulus, the last Roman emperor, was deposed by Odoacer in 476 and thus the Western empire came to a close. However, the eastern half continued with Constantinopolis as the capital city until its fall to the Turks in 1453: the Eastern, or Byzantine empire as it is known, thus forming a bridge between the ancient and modern worlds. By the time of the fall of Rome, Christianity had made its first definite and official mark upon the coinages of the world. This had come about mainly by a process of gradual development and evolution rather than by abrupt change, but it had come to stay and the Christian symbolism and connections which followed in the Byzantine empire and in different parts of Europe will next be considered.

35 The cross seen as 'The Salvation of the World' (SALVS MVNDI) on the reverse of a gold solidus struck by the Emperor Olybrius at Rome in AD 472.

4

DEVELOPMENTS IN
THE EAST AND WEST

There is no agreed date that can be placed as the commencement of what is known as the Byzantine empire. When Constantinopolis was founded by Constantine the Great in 330, his new capital city of the east was, in effect, little more than a moving of the centre of the Roman empire from Rome itself, but the gap between the old and the new capital cities and the two halves of the empire grew ever wider as the years passed until separation came about. The Western empire was soon to fall, but it is customary to date the commencement of the Byzantine coin series not from this event, but rather from the death of Theodosius the Great in 395, or from the reforms of the coinage made by Anastasius in 498. Thus, from the numismatic standpoint, the coin of the Eastern emperor Marcian already mentioned (the first to portray the figure of Christ) might be considered by some numismatists to belong to the early Byzantine coin series rather than the late Roman.

The early emperors of the Eastern empire, however, continued the monetary traditions established at Rome during the fourth century, and thus the types and coins show little change. The considerable reforms made by Anastasius in 498 set the Byzantine coinage upon a course of its own and, with the new coins and denominations, new types begin to appear. The

36 Reverse of a silver half-siliqua of Tiberius II (AD 578–582) with the cross and inscription identifying it as 'The Light of the World'. Struck at Carthage, North Africa.

Byzantine gold coins, bezants as they came to be known, circulated far and wide, and these, with bronze coins which were struck in large numbers, were those mainly used, as silver was not employed to a great extent. Christian types are in evidence at all periods, this being a continuation of the tradition established at Rome; and amongst the early types, Victory holding a long cross, and the cross of Christ, appear very frequently. During the reign of Tiberius II (578–582) the inscription LVX MVNDI ('The Light of the World') appears around a cross on some silver coins (**36**) and, also, the cross on steps first appears. Justinian II during his first reign (685–695) styles himself as SERVUS CHRISTI ('The servant of Christ') and on the obverse of his second reign coins (705–711) the bust of Christ is introduced as a new type (**37**), with the inscription IHS. CHRISTOS REX REGNANTIUM ('Jesus Christ, King of Kings'). It would appear very strange that this description of the emperor and the new type should have been introduced by one who was exiled on account of his cruelty to his subjects. On the coins Christ is depicted with a flowing beard and hair, His right hand is raised, in His left hand He holds the book of the Gospels, and behind His head are seen the arms of the cross.

37 The bust of Christ with the cross behind his head takes the dominant obverse position on gold solidi of Justinian II during his second reign (AD 705–711). Mint of Constantinople.

On some specimens Christ is shown as a much younger man with short beard and curly hair in an idealised style. It is impossible to tell whether these coins show the appearance of Christ as He was during His earthly lifetime as no authoritative contemporary description or picture of His features is known. From written records such as those of John of Damascus and Nicephorus Callisti, amongst other details it is suggested that He was bearded, and this is in agreement with what is possibly the oldest known painting of Christ in existence which is to be found on the ceiling of the catacomb of Domitilla in Rome. The portraiture of the Byzantine emperors themselves on their coins was merely representational, apart from a few isolated instances when it seems that an attempt was made to produce realistic portraiture. Accordingly, it must be considered that these coin portraits of Christ can have been given nothing more than similar treatment and cannot, therefore, be relied upon as adding evidence as to His appearance in person. It must be admitted that in the case of the first, 'older' head, portrait of Christ, the treatment is slightly more realistic than the contemporary coin portraits of Justinian and may point to the fact of the die engraver having an earlier sculpture or sketch of Christ on which to base his work.

A new departure as a type was made under Leo VI (886–912) when the Virgin Mary was first depicted (**38**). The treatment of the type is tastefully executed, and no doubt of the attribution is left by the fact that the word MARIA is found over the head, and, on either side MP ΘY which are abbreviations for MHTHP ΘEOY ('Mother of God'). On various coins of this and later reigns, the Virgin appears with hands raised or out-

38 A gold solidus of Leo VI, the Wise (AD 886–912), has the Virgin Mary *orans* as the major obverse type; the emperor is relegated to the reverse. Mint of Constantinople.

39 The Virgin Mary holding the infant Christ before Her on the obverse of a gold tetarteron nomisma of Michael VII (AD 1071–78). Mint of Constantinople.

stretched; holding the infant Christ; or holding before Her the infant, whose nimbate head is depicted (**39**). Some coins of the series show Her crowning the emperor (**40**), and others depict the city of Constantinopolis within which is seen the bust of the Virgin with arms raised.

During the tenth century a series of bronze coins was introduced, their special feature being that the names of the emperors by whom they were isued are not shown. Several varieties of these anonymous bronzes were issued but all have a portrayal of Christ as the obverse type (**41**). The earliest issues have the reverse given over to the inscription – IHSUS XRISTUS BASILEU BASILE ('Jesus Christ, King of Kings'). Although this inscription is in Greek wording, the lettering is Roman (where there is variation between the Greek and Roman letter forms) with the exception of the X (the Greek *chi*) of XRISTUS. Later variations in the type of the reverse include the cross on steps; a Patriarchal or Latin cross; the bust of the Virgin, or the Virgin standing, but all are linked by the common obverse type. It has been a matter of some difficulty to allot these anonymous coins

40 The Virgin Mary crowns the standing figure of Romanus III (AD 1028–34) on the reverse of a gold stamenon nomisma. Mint of Constantinople.

41 Byzantine 'anonymous' bronze coin struck after *c.* AD 989
with Christ holding the Gospels as the obverse type and hailed
in the reverse inscription as 'Jesus Christ, King of Kings'.

to the emperors who issued them but, fortunately, many of the
coins of this particular series were overstruck on earlier coins
with different types and, at times, traces of the under types are
still visible. By close and careful study of this overstriking
students have established with considerable reliability the
sequence of the different varieties that are known, and that the
series was issued in and between the reigns of John I (969–976)
and Alexius I (1081–1118).

In addition to these representations of Christ, beardless
portraits are found from Manuel I (1143–80) and at times the
full figure is shown seated on a throne or standing, occasionally
accompanied by the inscription EMMANOVHΛ (Emmanuel).
At times Christ or the Virgin Mary are shown crowning
or blessing the emperor, and the Archangel Michael is also
depicted.

Following the lead given by the Lombardic kings, which
will be mentioned later, representations of saints of the Christian Church are soon to be found employed as coin types;
they include Andronicus, Demetrius, George, Michael, and
Theodore.

Turning back again to earlier times, it can be seen that
Christianity made an impact on coinages other than those of
the Roman empire; probably the earliest instance being the
kingdom of Axum which flourished from about the first
century BC. The foundations of the kingdom were probably

laid by the Sabaeans – a South Arabian people who traced their descent from King Solomon – and it is the forerunner of modern Ethiopa. About 330 Christianity was established in Axum and the king, Ezanas, and his twin brother who ruled with and after him, were baptised into the faith. Coins are recorded from earlier kings such as Endybis (*c.* 250–275) and pride of place on the types above the head of the kings is given to the Sabaean symbol, the crescent and star. After the adoption of Christianity (*c.* 330) the crescent and star were replaced by the cross and within a few years the cross is found as the main type in the centre of the reverse of the coins (**42**).

Meanwhile, in Italy, following the downfall of the Roman Empire, new coinages began to emerge amongst the barbarian peoples who spread from the East. The Ostrogoths, Lombards, Visigoths, Burgundians and Franks each produced coinages – mainly of gold – which were more or less copies of late Roman or Byzantine prototypes; thus the cross and other Christian symbols appear. At first these may well have had little significance, but as Christianity was gradually adopted by these barbarian peoples, the fundamental reasons for the employment of such types may well have become more evident to them.

On the Ostrogothic coinages of the sixth century the letters ND standing for NOMINE DOMINE ('In the name of God') appear, and the first representation of a saint as a coin type seems to have been introduced by the Lombardic king Cunincpert (688–700). The standing figure of St Michael is found on his coins and there can be no doubt of the correctness of this attribution

42   The small gold coins of the Axumite Kingdom of Abyssinia incorporate a cross in their reverse designs after the conversion of King Ezanas to Christianity about AD 330. This is almost the earliest use of the Christian cross on coinage and certainly the most regular.

43 The gold solidi of the Lombardic king Cunincpert (AD 688–700) closely follow Late Roman prototypes and the Saint, Michael, depicted on the reverse appears to be the first instance of a saint used as a coin type.

of the type as, once again, the name of the figure depicted is given in the inscription (**43**). The coins of the Franks from the time of Clovis who founded the Merovingian dynasty, and who was baptised into the Christian faith on Christmas Day 496, became the currency of the whole of Gaul as the Frankish kingdom in the north of the country was extended. The coinages were produced not only on account of the kings, but also on behalf of feudal lords and Church dignitaries, and thus the Church became interested in the issue of coins from which a profit was made, this interest remaining for a considerable period and assuming important proportions. The patriarchs, or popes of Rome themselves, who had remained a steady and dominant factor from late Roman times and throughout the barbaric period, struck coins from the time of Pope Adrian I (772–795) and have continued to do so (with brief exceptions) until the present day.

5

ENTER ENGLAND

With Christianity established in Gaul under the Merovingians and with commercial contact between Gaul and Anglo-Saxon England, it may be expected that the second coming of Christianity to these islands would not be far away. The Christianity introduced to Britain by the Romans in the fourth century had been almost extinguished during the Dark Ages, but with the coming of Augustine who was sent to England in 597 by Pope Gregory, and who later became the first archbishop of Canterbury, the story really begins afresh.

The history of coinage in Britain begins far away in northern Greece when Philip II of Macedon (359–336 BC) struck some very fine gold staters which depicted on the obverse the head of Apollo and, on the reverse, above the name of the king, a two-horse chariot. These coins proved to be very popular and they became known and used in central Europe where the inhabitants started to make copies of them in considerable numbers but of degenerate style. As the use of these types spread even further west into Gaul and then across the Channel into Britain, so the style became even more barbaric. The earliest British coins were therefore exceedingly crude copies in gold of the beautiful Macedonian prototypes, the date of their introduction being possibly in the early part of the first century

BC. The use of coinage spread amongst many of the tribes inhabiting Britain and, later in the first century, gold coins of varied types began to be struck; small quantities were also struck in silver and in copper.

With the coming of the Romans, the Roman coinage superseded the native issues and thus became the normal currency throughout the occupation. Roman mints were established during the late third century at Londinium (London) and also probably at Camulodunum (Colchester), although the exact location of this second mint is slightly uncertain. During the Dark Ages crude copies of late Roman coins met the currency requirements of Britain until a new Anglo-Saxon coinage emerged towards the close of the sixth century. A most interesting numismatic relic of the early beginnings of the second coming of Christianity survives, dated even before the arrival of Augustine. Aethelberht, king of Kent, about the year 560 married Berchta, a great grand-daughter of the Merovingian king Clovis and, being a Christian, Berchta brought with her to England Bishop Luidhard as her chaplain. During the nineteenth century a small hoard of coins and other objects was found in the churchyard of St Martin's Canterbury, the church (or a slightly earlier building) in which Berchta used to worship and which has been described as 'the most ancient place of Christian worship in England'. Amongst this hoard was included a gold piece – probably more of a medalet than a coin – and this has now been attributed with reasonable certainty to Bishop Luidhard. On the obverse there is a bust representing the bishop around which is the inscription now read as LEVDARDVS EPS, and on the reverse, a double cross; it is more than probable that the piece was actually struck at Canterbury.

The first Anglo-Saxon coinages were designed mainly from Merovingian and Byzantine prototypes and thus, following the established traditions, these gold thrymsas, as they are known, employ the cross as a frequent type. The fact that the crude busts which are to be found on the obverses are often shown accompanied by a cross or staff, gives rise to the theory that Church dignitaries in England may well have had something to do with their issue. The gold coinage was soon surplanted by similar coins but struck in silver, which are generally known as sceatta although the actual name of the coins is uncertain. Many varieties of type are to be found in this group of coins and a cross is on some pieces combined with a bird which may well be symbolic of the Holy Dove. London and Canterbury appear to have been the main places of mintage of the silver sceatta.

Although in southern England a new coin, the silver penny, replaced the sceat coinage (**44**), as will be mentioned below, in Northumbria the coinage was continued first in base silver and then in copper (the latter coins at times being referred to as stycas). The Northumbrian sceat coinage as a separate issue was introduced by King Eadberht (737–758) and was continued for about 100 years. The types of the coins consist in the main simply of the name of the king on the obverse and that of the moneyer on the reverse, around, in each case, a cross, pellet, annulet, or other similar device. A coin formerly attributed to King Ecgfrith, well known for his patronage of the church, and which depicted on the reverse a cross surrounded by rays of light and the letters LVXX (light), is now treated with considerable suspicion as to its being genuine. The plain cross frequently appears as the motif in the centre of many coins and during the second reign of Aethelred I (789–796) an interesting sceat may depict a shrine with lettering which has been suggested to be an abbreviation of SANCTVS CVTHBERTVS.

The first coins of the English series definitely known to have been struck by a church authority form part of this Northumbrian group. These coins were struck by Ecgberht, archbishop

44 Anglo-Saxon silver sceat *c*. AD 720–730 with a reverse type of a standing figure holding two crosses. Although the design is almost certainly derived from a Byzantine prototype it may have been adapted for use by an early church dignitary.

45 Bronze sceat of Archbishop Ecgberht of York (AD 732/4–766) with a mitred figure holding two crosses.

of York (732/4–766), and from this point of time the church retained an interest in a number of coinages until the reign of Henry VIII. Ecgberht's coins follow the normal pattern of the regal issues having on the obverse the name of the archbishop followed by the letters AR, being an abbreviation of his title ARCHIEPISCOPUS; on the reverse is the name of the moneyer with, in the centre of each side, a cross, annulet, or similar motif. One coin has a reverse type with a mitred figure holding a cross and crosier (some dies show two crosses) which is undoubtedly a representation of the archbishop himself (**45**). A remarkable coin amongst the issues of the archbishops of York, which otherwise consist almost entirely of copper stycas (**46**), is a unique gold solidus of Archbishop Wigmund (837–854?) in the British Museum (**47**). This coin is of very fine workmanship; it has on the obverse a tonsured bust of Wigmund and on the reverse a cross with the inscription MVNVS DIVINVM. The interpretation of the type can therefore hardly be less than 'The Cross, the Gift of God'. Although a number of students have cast suspicion on this coin, it now appears to be genuine, although from an issue (possibly for a religious occasion) unusual for the period. With Wigmund's successor, Wulfhere (854–900?), this early series of coins of the archbishops of York came to a close.

On the Continent, as in England, silver coinages had re-

46   Bronze styca of Archbishop Wigmund of York (AD 837–854?) with his name on the obverse and the name of the moneyer, Edilveard, on the reverse, each around a cross.

47 Unique gold solidus of Archbishop Wigmund of York (AD 837–854?) with his facing bust on the obverse and the legend MVNVS DIVINUM around a cross on the reverse.

placed the earlier gold issues and an entirely new coin was introduced by Pepin the Short (751–768). This was a larger and thinner silver piece known as the denier, a name which was derived from the Roman denarius, and it was to become almost universally imitated throughout Europe for many years. There is little doubt that the prototype of these new thinner coins is to be found in the Sassanian coins which will be mentioned at the end of this chapter. The denier, or silver penny as it is known, was introduced into England possibly about 775 by one of the kings of Kent, or by Offa, king of Mercia (757–796). Even if Offa was not responsible for the actual introduction of the new coin, he certainly popularised the use of it and he struck it in considerable quantities and varieties of types although his coins are now very rare. Many of his early coins show a portrait bust representative of the king, and although in some instances the style tends to be somewhat crude, a few early dies are very artistic. The name of the moneyer appears frequently on the reverse around some form of central motif which is often in the form of a plain or ornamental cross. From about 792 Offa's pennies were struck slightly wider in diameter and without the portrait. A few coins show the name of Eadberht and this may possibly be the bishop of London of that name who died about 788 and, if so, it is the only appearance of the bishops of London on the coinage, unless some of the early anonymous coins were struck by them.

During the reign of Offa the archbishops of Canterbury began to coin, although it is highly possible that they had taken part in the issue of the earlier anonymous thrymsas and sceatta.

Archbishop Jaenberht (766–792) inaugurated the series and his name appears on his coins together with that of Offa as overlord. His title AREP appears after his name. Aethelheard, who succeeded Jaenberht, is described as PONT(IFEX) (Pontif) on the coins of his first issue during which he introduced the Chi-Rho as a type, but after his consecration in 793 he is styled as ARCEPI. The title is expanded on a coin of Wulfred (805–832) which reads VVLFREDI ARCHIEPISCOPI and the archbishop employed a facing bust of himself as the obverse type, this probably having been prompted by a portrait of Pope Adrian I on a coin issued a few years earlier. Amongst the varied reverse types on his coins, Wulfred introduced the alpha and omega monogram. Archbishop Ceolnoth (833–870) had a tonsured bust (himself?) represented on the obverse and a Chi-Rho monogram with the moneyer's name on the reverse (**48**). The last name of an archbishop of Canterbury found on the coins of this early series is that of Plegmund (890–914), and some of his coins have three letters in the centre of the reverse. Brooke reads these as XPF (for possibly XPS – 'Christos'), but Oman, on the other hand, reads them as XDF standing for CHRISTUS DEI FILIUS ('Christ the Son of God'). Which of these readings is correct – if either – remains uncertain.

Very rare coins (five only being recorded) which carry the name of the Apostle, Andrew, were issued by Ecgberth, king of Wessex (802–839) and have been attributed to an ecclesiastical mint at Rochester. On one die the inscription SCS ANDREAS APO is completed by STOLVS being placed in the centre of the

48 Silver penny of Archbishop Ceolnoth of Canterbury (AD 833–870) with a tonsured bust on the obverse and the moneyer's name (WUNHERE) around the Chi-Rho monogram on the reverse.

reverse, this being replaced on another die by the alpha and omega monogram. The attribution to Rochester is enhanced by the fact that the cathedral there was dedicated to St Andrew. It is known from coins of the Mercian king, Ceolwulf I (821–823) that a mint was operative there which inscribed them with the ancient name of the city DOROBREBIA. Ceolwulf I was one of the kings of the period who also used the alpha and omega monogram as a type on their regal coins.

An interesting new inscription appeared in France on the deniers of Louis le Debonnaire (814–840) which portrayed a round temple or church surmounted by a cross and around which is the wording XPISTIANA RELIGIO ('The Christian Religion'). Temples of various types had appeared on many occasions on the coins of the Greek and Roman series, but in this new appearance the inscription leaves no doubt that the building shown is a representation of a Christian place of worship (**49**). These coins were without doubt the prototype

49 Silver denier of Louis le Debonnaire (AD 814–840) with the King's name around a cross and the legend reading 'The Christian Religion' around a representation of a temple or church on the reverse.

of coins of Edward the Elder (899–924), king of Wessex, which show as the reverse type a representation which is obviously a Christian church of which the tower, nave, and the side aisles are seen (**50**). In this instance, however, there is no inscription to confirm the type. This reign also introduces in the Anglo-Saxon series the Hand of Providence which is seen descending from the clouds and giving the sign of Benediction, and another type which shows a bird holding a twig in its beak has been suggested as representing the dove sent out from the ark by Noah (Genesis 8:8).

50   Silver penny of Edward the Elder (AD 899–924) with an Anglo-Saxon church shown above the moneyer's name VVLFGAR on the reverse.

At about the same time memorial coins were struck in East Anglia in the name of St Eadmund, the murdered East Anglian king (**51**); at York in the name of St Peter, and at Lincoln with that of St Martin. Other coins show the inscriptions MIRABILIA FECIT ('He hath done marvellous things') and D(OMI)N(U)S D(EU)S REX) ('O Lord God (Heavenly) King') which are obviously of Christian significance. All the coins of this group were struck, almost certainly, by the Danish invaders (*c*. AD 890–*c*. 910) who had settled in England.

The later Anglo-Saxon coinage may be said to commence with the reign of Aethelstan (924–939) who was able to style himself on his coins as King of all Britain. Aethelstan issued a decree that there should be only one money used throughout the land and this single coinage was maintained until and after the Norman Conquest when William the Conqueror made little change in it, apart from his name appearing in place of that of Harold II, this being the greatest compliment William could pay to the late Anglo-Saxon coinage which was renowned throughout Europe for good weight and quality of metal. A number of mints had been established in different parts of the

51   Silver memorial penny for St Eadmund, viking coinage of Danish East Anglia, *c*. AD 890–910. The reverse legend is SCEADMYN around A (= Anglorum).

country; by the time of Aethelred II some seventy were in operation and the name of the moneyer and mint at which the coin was struck became customary as the reverse inscription. Also, a cross was normally placed at the beginning of the inscriptions on both sides of the coin, a feature often found on the coins struck during the centuries which followed. It is highly possible that some of the coins of this period were struck on behalf of various ecclesiastical authorities but, as no special marks were placed on the coins, such issues cannot now be distinguished. However, one possible exception to this may be the very rare coins of Edward the Martyr (975–978) struck at the Stamford mint which have an annulet on the reverse. It has been suggested that these specially marked coins were struck on behalf of the abbot of Medeshamstede (Peterborough).

Under Aethelred II, the Unready (978–1016) the Hand of Providence appears once again (**52**). On some dies the Hand is shown giving the sign of Benediction, and again on others, between the letters alpha and omega. Another coin of obvious Christian type from this reign is one of extreme rarity and on the obverse is seen the Holy Lamb of God, nimbate, and a banner of crucifix form (**53**). The letters AGN in the field standing for AGNUS DEI (Lamb of God) leave no doubt of the meaning of the type and the reverse normally to be found coupled with this obverse shows the Holy Dove with wings outstretched. Some numismatists considered these types to have been introduced in connection with the millennium, but modern opinion is that the types were introduced as one of the

52   Silver penny of Aethelred II (AD 978–1016) with the king's name and bust on the obverse and the Hand of God between A and ω (alpha and omega) on the reverse, together with the name of the moneyer and mint – EALHSTAN MO LVN(don).

53   Very rare silver penny of Aethelred II (AD 978–1016) with a nimbate Agnus Dei on the obverse and, on the reverse, the Holy Dove.

changes that were made every few years and that the innovation did not find favour, hence the types were replaced by others of a more customary character showing the royal portrait.

During the Norman and early Plantagenet periods little basic change was made in the scheme of coinage and the silver penny remained the standard and virtually the only coin to be struck. There was a feeling, however, for an expanded range of denominations in the coinage and in 1279 under Edward I halfpennies and farthings were introduced, as well as a small issue of short duration of a larger coin, the groat, which was equal to four pennies. Pennies of gold and halfpennies of silver had been struck very occasionally in the earlier periods, but were exceptional.

An addition was made to the normal style of obverse inscriptions by Eudes, king of France (887–898) who struck deniers with the words DEI GRATIA REX ('King, by the Grace of God') following his name. This claim will have had no little significance in those early and unsettled times and the formula became widely used throughout Europe. In England it was used on the seals of the realm from the time of William I but it made its first appearance on a coin with the groats of Edward I and came into general use under Edward III. It is now to be found on many of the world's coinages to modern times.

By the time that the period of the supremacy of the denier and its English equivalent, the silver penny, drew to a close, many of the coins were struck by or on behalf of Church dignitaries in various parts of Europe. In England, the issues of the archbishops of Canterbury and York have been mentioned

54 Silver penny of Edward I (1272–1307) struck by the moneyer Robert de Hadeleie for the abbot of St Edmundsbury. A plain cross is seen above the king's crown on the obverse.

together with a possible issue by a bishop of London; other ecclesiastical issues are known of the bishops of Durham and the abbots of St Edmundsbury and, possibly, Reading. With a more centralised policy of mint control introduced by Edward I with his new coinage of 1279, the name of the moneyer was no longer necessary on the coins and from that time the name of the mint appears by itself. The one exception to this is provided by the coins of the abbot of St Edmundsbury on which the name of his moneyer, Robert de Hadeleie (**54**), was retained until about 1284 after which the coins of the mint conformed to the normal practice.

The names of the church dignitaries themselves did not appear from the time of Plegmund of Canterbury but on the coins of Edward I and Edward II, in some instances, marks were introduced to distinguish the ecclesiastical from the regal issues. The York coins of the archbishops' mint have a quatrefoil in the centre of the long cross on the reverse, although the Canterbury coins show no special marks. At Durham a cross moline marks the coins of Bishop Bek (**55**); one end of the long

55 Silver penny of Bishop Bek of Durham (1284–1311) struck under Edward I. Note the cross moline above the crown instead of the usual plain cross.

56   Silver penny of Bishop Kellawe of Durham (1311–16)
struck under Edward II (1307–27). A crosier head terminates
the vertical arm of the cross.

cross on the reverse finishing as a crosier head marks the coins
of his successor Bishop Kellawe (**56**); and then a lion rampant
was used for Bishop Beaumont. As the dates of these various
bishops are recorded, these Durham coins are first class evidence for the dating and sequence of the various minor varieties of detail that are found on them and on regal coins from
other mints when such coins exhibit these same minor features. For example, the varied abbreviations in the spelling of
the king's name – EDW, EDWA, etc.; the shape of his crown, and
varieties in the actual shape of the letters of the inscription.

Before passing on from this period, brief mention should be
made of the development of the coinages of the lands of the
Middle East and India, although they follow a tradition uncon-
nected with the main theme of this book. Following the break-
up of the vast empire of Alexander the Great, the Parthians
were one of the peoples who soon declared their independence;
their coinages were based upon the Greek system with
drachms and tetradrachms of silver and copper coins of uncertain denominations. With the Sassanian dynasty which followed the Parthians, the drachms (or dirhems) began to be
struck on much thinner and wider flans. These thinner coins
undoubtedly provided the prototype for the European silver
pennies but, as they were of lighter weight, they were of
smaller diameter. The normal types of the Sassanian drachms
consisted of a portrait of the king on the obverse, and on the
reverse the fire altar and two attendants associated with the
Zoroastrian faith (**57**).

A further important development in world history commenced in the seventh century AD with the conquests of the

57 Sassanian silver dirhem of Hormazd IV (AD 579–590), struck at Raiy. It has a crowned bust of the king and a Zoroastrian fire altar with two attendants.

Arabs over parts of the Byzantine empire and the whole of Persia. At first the Arabs struck coins resembling the current Byzantine and Sassanian types but with the addition of the names of governors or mints in Arabic script.

With the rise and teaching of Mohammed, the faith of Islam was born and soon gained many followers. The coins issued by the many Islamic rulers seldom carried pictorial types and, following the Islamic tradition, the obverses and reverses were normally taken up by inscriptions in Arabic. Although there were many variations in the inscriptions in the long series of Islamic coins, the name of the ruler and mint are found in a number of instances and, most frequently, the Kalimah, the Islamic profession of faith which, transliterated and translated reads, '*la ilah illa Allah wahdahu la sherik lahu Mohammed rasul Allah*' – 'There is no God but Allah, who has no associate: Mohammed is the Prophet of Allah' (**58**). Many other inscriptions of a religious character are also to be found and many of the coins are dated by the Hegira era – the flight of Mohammed on 15 July AD 622 from Mecca to Medina.

In India an indigenous coinage probably commenced in the sixth century BC and the coins were flat, plate-like pieces of metal into which a number of punch marks were impressed (**59**). Although a few coins were struck in copper in the years which followed, they were mainly of silver and among many different punch marks which are known, Buddhist symbols are included. Following the invasions of the

58   Silver dirhem of the Abbasid Caliph Al Mansur (AD 754–775), struck at Baghdad. The Kalimah, the Islamic profession of faith, begins in the centre of the obverse and is completed in the centre of the reverse.

Greeks under Alexander the Great, the Sakas, and the Kushans, the coins struck by them followed their own traditions of types and representations of many deities are to be found. With the rise of the Gupta dynasty in the fourth century AD and the revival of Hinduism, many of the fine coins struck have types associated with the Hindu faith and rites. A complete change from pictorial to inscriptional types occurred with the Muslim invasion of India which, although it commenced in AD 712 in Sind, took place mainly in the eleventh century. The coins then followed the normal Islamic pattern of issues elsewhere, the inscriptions on many of the coins of the long series containing religious sentences of varied nature. The evidence of Christian types on Indian coins is very limited. However, on the coins of Portuguese India from 1511, the cross does appear following the tradition of its appearance on the coins of Portugal itself and, during the period 1580–1650, portraits of St Philip and St John are encountered.

59   Indian punch-marked silver karshapana, c. 216–207 BC. Amongst the punch marks, top right, are traces of a Buddhist stupa.

6

THE EXPANSION
OF THE COINAGE

From the preceding chapter it will be seen that during the period under discussion, the silver penny, since the time of its introduction, was almost the only denomination struck in Europe. In the twelfth century a desire was felt for a fuller and more serviceable coinage to meet the demands of expanding trade and in Venice, under Doge Enrico Dandolo (1192–1205), a larger silver coin was struck known as a grosso, or great coin. The Venetians employed Christian types for their grosso (**60**); on the obverse there is a representation of the Doge receiving a banner from St Mark, the patron saint of the city, and on the reverse is a figure of Christ, enthroned and nimbate, the idea undoubtedly copied from the earlier Byzantine coins of similar type.

60 Venetian silver grosso of Doge Giovanni Soranzo (1312–28). The types, introduced by Doge Enrico Dandolo, show St Mark and the Doge, and Christ enthroned facing.

Further east another important coinage appeared a few years before the Venetian grosso, struck by the Armenian people who had migrated to Cilicia in the eleventh century. Armenia holds the distinction of being the first country to adopt Christianity as the state religion , in 303, some ten years earlier than the Edict of Milan which gave freedom of worship to the Christians in the Roman empire. Levon I, the first king of the Cilician Armenians, issued coinage soon after 1196 consisting of silver coins slightly heavier in weight than the Venetian grosso with, in addition, pieces of double the size and weight (**61**); these pre-dated the introduction of coins larger than the silver penny in Europe. On the obverse of these fine coins Levon is depicted enthroned, the foreparts of lions being seen on either side of the throne, a feature which can be traced back to the throne of Solomon (1 Kings 10:19). A crowned lion holding a cross is the reverse type and from this issue to the end of the series in 1375, a cross of one style or another was always featured on the coins. The state religion was a treasured possession of the Armenians and Christianity was immediately reflected on their coinage as the Armenian script inscriptions on Levon's coins can be translated 'Levon King of the Hayots [Armenians] Through the Power of God'. When Levon was annointed and crowned king in the cathedral in Tarsus in 1198, a second series of coins appeared in celebration of this event (**62**); the obverse depicts Levon kneeling before Christ with, between them, the Holy Dove or rays of light descending from Heaven. On the reverse of Levon's copper tanks,

61   Silver double tram of Levon I (1199–1219) of Cilician Armenia with the king enthroned and a lion holding a cross on the reverse.

62 Silver coronation tram of Levon I with the obverse type of the king kneeling before Christ and rays of light between them.

which are coins of good size, the cross on steps formed the central type, this again having been copied from the earlier Byzantine appearance of this feature. On the death of Levon in 1219 his sole heir was a daughter, Zabel, then only three years of age. After a brief marriage which ended about 1224 with the death of her husband, Zabel was soon married to Hetoum, the son of Gosdantin who was one of her regents, and on their trams Hetoum and Zabel are depicted holding a cross and with the inscription 'Power is to God' (**63**). Finally, one further coin in the Armenian series should be mentioned, struck by Oshin, king from 1308 to 1320. Probably the number issued of these coins was small as they are now very rare. On the obverse Oshin is shown enthroned and by his left shoulder is seen the Hand of God in blessing; the issue was probably in celebration of his coronation.

The Venetian grosso was soon imitated in other parts of Europe and during the years which followed a very wide variety of types are to be found. Outside Venice the denomination was first coined in France by Louis IX in 1266 and the reverse type of this coin shows a representation of the abbey

63 Obverse of a silver tram of Zabel (daughter of Levon I) and her husband Hetoum; both standing holding a cross between them.

64   Silver gros tournois of Louis IX of France (1226–70) with a reverse type showing the Abbey of St Martin at Tours.

of St Martin at Tours, which became an important seat of coinage. The coin itself became known as the gros tournois (**64**). Although, as mentioned, the groat was introduced into the English coinage by Edward I in 1279, its first appearance was of very brief duration and the denomination remained in abeyance until 1351 (**65**).

Gold coins returned to regular use at Florence in 1252 with the issue of the florin which depicts the standing figure of St John the Baptist on the obverse and a lily on the reverse (**66**). As was the case with the Venetian grosso, the Florentine gold coins were soon imitated at other mints and in some instances even the actual types were copied.

To meet the need for a coinage of higher denominations resultant upon the rise of prices and wages following the Black Death, Edward III introduced in January 1344 a coinage in gold (the first regular gold coinage in England) and on the reverse of the coins he added for legends (or inscriptions) actual passages

65   Silver groat (four pence) of Edward III (1327–77) of the basic type that remained in use until about 1504. Struck at London (CIVITAS LONDON). The inscription is POSVI DEUM ADIVTOREM MEVM (I have made God my Helper).

66   Gold florin of Florence with the standing figure of John the Baptist as the main type and a lily on the reverse.

from Scriptures or sentences of Christian significance. The largest coin of the series was called a florin but it was twice the weight of the Italian coin and was current for seventy-two pence. On the obverse there is a representation of the king seated on the throne, beside which are lions (a feature mentioned on the coins of Levon I of Cilician Armenia, **61**) and around which are the king's name and titles (**67**). The reverse legend in abbreviated form is IESUS AUTUM TRANSIENS PER MEDIUM ILLORUM IBAT ('But Jesus, passing through the midst of them went his way': Luke 4:30), this having been used for many years as a talisman for preservation in battle. The 'leopard', or half-florin, was so called because of the obverse type of a lion (leopard being the French heraldic term for a lion passant guardant) bearing a banner emblazoned with the royal arms quartering the English lions with the French lilies because Edward lay claim to the throne of France. The legend is DOMINE NE IN FURORE TUO ARGUAS ME ('O Lord rebuke not in Thine anger': Psalm 6:1). The 'helm', or quarter-florin, has the

67   Gold florin (also called a double leopard) of Edward III (1327–77), introduced in January 1344.

legend EXALTABITUR IN GLORIA ('he shall be exalted in glory')
and a lion standing on a helmet as the obverse type. Having had
only a very brief life, the coins of this issue are very rare, seven
specimens in all being recorded. They were replaced in August
1344 by a new issue of gold coins, the largest coin, the noble,
being slightly heavier than the florin and current for eighty
pence (**68**). The obverse depicts the king within a ship and it is
thought the type may be commemorative of the victory over
the French at the battle of Sluys in 1340. The king is seen
holding a sword and a shield emblazoned with the royal arms
and the legend is the same as used on the florin. The half-noble
is of similar type and legend, and the quarter-noble, depicting
only the royal shield of arms, uses the 'Exaltabitur' legend of
the helm. On a few dies for the half-nobles, the word NE is
omitted from the legend which therefore reads 'O Lord,
rebuke me in Thine anger'; hence they are commonly referred
to as the cursing half-nobles.

Under Edward IV the currency value of the noble was
increased to 120 pence and it became known as the ryal. A new
coin, current for the eighty pence of the old noble but, of
course, of lighter weight, was then introduced and has the
legend PER CRUCEM TUAM SALVA NOS CHRISTE REDEMPTOR ('By
Thy cross, save us, O Christ our Redeemer'). The obverse
type of this new coin is St Michael slaying the dragon (Revelation 12:7), and the type was responsible for the name by which
the coin was known – the angel (**69**). On the half-angels the

68   Gold noble of Edward III (1327–77), introduced in August
1344.

69   Gold angel of Henry VIII (1509–47) with the archangel St
Michael slaying the dragon as the obverse type, first introduced
by Edward IV and giving the coin its name.

legend was O CRUX AVE SPES UNICA ('Hail, O Cross, our only
hope').

The conventional representational facing portrait of the king
on the silver coins, which had become customary from the
time of Edward I, was replaced by Henry VII about 1504 by a
real profile portrait of himself. Even so, his son, Henry VIII,
retained his father's portrait on his coins for the first seventeen
years of his reign.

It will be remembered that the coins of the ecclesiastical
mints in England began to show special marks during the reign
of Edward I. This practice was continued at times until late in
the reign of Henry VI when the letter B appeared, the initial
letter of the name of Bishop Lawrence Booth of Durham
(1457–62 and 1464–76). This innovation was copied at York
with the letter G for Archbishop George Nevill (1465–72 and
1475–6) and soon afterwards at Canterbury with M for Archbishop Morton (1486–1500); the letters were sometimes
accompanied by the personal marks of the issuers. The use of
the bishop's initial remained a normal feature until the closure
of the ecclesiastical mints.

In the charter granted by Edward IV to Archbishop Thomas
Bouchier of Canterbury in 1463 permission was granted for
the archbishop to strike half-groats and halfpence in addition
to the pennies which were the coins normally struck at the
privilege mints. In 1501 a similar right to strike half-groats was
granted to the archbishops of York, but Cardinal Wolsey went

a step further by striking groats, a denomination struck only at the royal mints. Cardinal Wolsey is encountered in the story of the coinage because, in his official position as Chancellor and administrator of the Tower mint, in 1526 he was ordered to introduce a re-organised scheme of coinage in reduced weights and fineness to bring the English into line with contemporary Continental coinages. Wolsey issued coins as bishop of Durham (1523–29) and as archbishop of York (1514–30). On coins of both mints his initials T W appear, together with his cardinal's hat as his personal mark which is placed under the royal shield on the reverse of the coins. A notable feature of Wolsey's York coins is that they include the groat (**70**), this being the only instance of a coin of this denomination struck at one of the privilege mints. The dies from which the groats were struck were similar to those for the regal coins, hence their issue must have had some sort of official approval. However, when Wolsey fell out with the king, these groats would have figured against him had he lived to stand trial after his downfall and arrest at York in 1530 for high treason. The placing of his cardinal's hat under the king's arms appears to have been the principal cause of the trouble, the wording of the indictment reading, 'Also the said lord cardinal of his further pompous and presumptious mind, hath enterprised to join and imprint the cardinal's hat under your arms in your coin of groats, made at your city of York, which like deed hath not yet been seen to have been done by any subject within your realm before this time'.

70   Silver groat of Henry VIII (1509–47) struck by Archbishop Wolsey of York. The king is represented as a young man and, on the reverse, the royal shield is flanked by Wolsey's initials, TW, and has his cardinal's hat below it.

It was no doubt during Thomas Cromwell's administration and about the time of the dissolution of the monasteries that the ecclesiastical coinages came to an end (probably in 1534), and thus concluded an interesting chapter in the history of English numismatics. The usefulness and importance of these mints and their coins to the student of this series cannot be over-estimated as in so many cases the coins can be dated closely on account of the special marks or initials found on them. This, as mentioned earlier, has enabled other coins of similar style and detail, but which do not show the special marks, to be dated or grouped around the ecclesiastical issues.

Apart from the appearance of St Michael on the English angels and St George on horseback slaying the dragon on some very rare gold coins struck by Henry VIII (therefore known as the George nobles and half-nobles), the only Christian refer-ences on coins of the period are to be found in the reverse legends. Several different scriptural quotations were employed but none were more appropriate than those to be found on the coins of James I (see below).

Mention should be made of the ceremony of the king touching people to cure scrofula, an infection of the skin. The custom, obviously linked with religious significance, was instituted in France by Robert II (996–1017) and in England by Edward the Confessor (1042–66) who, it was said, cured a young girl's disease by making the sign of the Cross several times over the infection. Edward I gave a gift of one penny to those who came to him to be touched, with an extra seven pence to those who were particularly poor. King Henry VII created a special church service at which the touching for the King's Evil, as it was called, took place and the gift, a memento rather than a charity, was an angel which had the very appropriate type of St Michael slaying the dragon and the legend PER CRUCEM TUAM SALVA NOS, CHRISTE REDEMPTOR ('By Thy Cross save us, O Christ our Redeemer'). A special 'Healing Service' was included in the English Church Prayer Book of Henry VIII and, under Mary Tudor, the legend was changed on the angels to another most appropriate quotation, A DOMINO FACTUM EST ISTUD ET EST MIRABILE IN OCULIS NOSTRI

('This is the Lord's doing, and it is miraculous in our eyes':
Psalm 118:23). Many of the angels surviving today are pierced
with a small round hole because they were suspended on a
white ribbon and hung around the sufferer's neck in the
ceremony by the sovereign. When the angel ceased to be
struck, after the restoration of Charles II in 1660, medalettes
were produced and used in their place; these continued to be
made until 1807 but were not coins and had no currency value.
In England Queen Anne was the last sovereign to touch for the
'King's Evil'. The custom continued in France until 1775 when
Louis XVI touched over 2000 people with, it is reported,
considerable success.

At this point attention should now be turned to the coinage
of Scotland which followed a somewhat similar pattern to that
of England. Commencing with silver pennies of David I
(1124–53) a cross of varied nature formed the central type on
the reverse of the coins; this was surrounded by an inscription
giving the name of the moneyer and mint. In the second
coinage of David II (1357–67) there was an expansion of the
coinage when a gold noble current for eighty pence was
introduced. The types copied those of the noble of Edward III
of England which had been struck a few years earlier and
employed the same reverse legend IHC TRANSIENS PER MEDIUM
ILLORUM IBAT. On the Scottish coins, which are very rare, the
Scottish arms – the lion rampant – replaced those of Edward III
on the English coin. On the companion groats and half-groats
issued at the same time, a profile portrait was used, following
the lead of many of the earlier Scottish pennies, and the reverse
legend in abbreviated form was DOMINUS PROTECTOR MEUS ET
LIBERATOR MEUS ('The Lord is my protector and deliverer').
Under Robert III (1390–1406) a new type appeared (**71**), St
Andrew on his cross being shown on the gold lion and
accompanied by the legend XPC REGNAT XPC VINCIT XPC IMP
('Christ rules, Christ conquers, Christ commands'), a legend
that had appeared on earlier coins of France. On the demy, the
smaller denomination, only the cross of St Andrew was used.
In this reign the English-type facing portrait replaced the
profile portrait on the silver coins, although some later issues
retained it.

71 Reverse of a gold lion of Robert III of Scotland (1390–1406) with St Andrew crucified on his saltire cross.

Other later scriptural or similar legends of Christian significance include SALVUM FAC POPULUM TUUM DOMINE ('Lord, save thy people': Psalm 28:10); EXURGAT DEUS ET DISSIPENTUR INIMICI EIUS ('Let God arise and let his enemies be scattered': Psalm 68:1); PER LIGNUM CRUCIS SALVI SUMUS ('We are saved through the wood of the Cross'); HONOR REGIS IUDUCIUM DILIGIT ('The king's strength loveth judgement': Psalm 99:4), and DILICIE DOMINI COR HUMILE ('A humble heart is the delight of the Lord'). However, when James VI of Scotland became James I of England following the death of Elizabeth I in 1603, the legend FACIAM EOS IN UNAM GENTEM ('I will make them one nation': Ezekiel 37:22) appeared and, most appropriately, QUAE DEUS CONIUNXIT NEMO SEPARET ('What God hath joined together let not man put asunder': Matthew 19:6) (**72**). This legend appeared on the contemporary coins of both Scotland and England. Similar style inscriptions remained in use until

72 Silver shilling of James I (1603–25) with the appropriate Biblical quotation on the reverse signifying his joint rule as James VI of Scotland and James I of England.

the end of the Scottish coinage in 1709, following the Union of the Parliaments of Scotland and England in 1707.

Mention should be made of a series of copper pennies and farthings which are not part of the normal Scottish coinage, a number of which were found at Crossraguel Abbey where, it was suggested, they were struck. A later and more probably correct attribution is that the pennies were struck by Bishop Kennedy who was granted the privilege of striking coins in 1452 and who died in 1465; if this is so, the coins are very closely dated. It is probable that St Andrews was the site of the mint as numbers of the pennies have been found in the district and the reverse inscription MONETA PAUPERUM ('money of the poor') suggests the reason for this unusual issue. The crowned orb is the obverse type of the pennies.

On the Continent much greater freedom and variation of type is met with and the types of Christian significance and implication are frequently to be found. Charles of Anjou (1266–85) issued for Naples a fine gold coin which portrays the Virgin Mary and the Archangel Gabriel (**73**); this type depicting the Annunciation (Luke 1:28) was copied in France where it continued for a long period. The Holy Lamb of God (John 1:29) appeared as the type on a gold coin introduced in France during the reign of Philip IV (1285–1314) and which was struck intermittently for over 100 years. The coin was known as the agnel or mouton (**74**). The Paschal Lamb is portrayed standing in front of a cross and pennon, around which is the legend AGNUS DEI, QUI TOLLIS PECCATA MUNDI, MISERERE NOBIS ('Lamb of God who takest away the sins of the world, have mercy upon

73 Reverse of a gold salute of Charles of Anjou, King of Naples (1266–85) showing the Virgin Mary with the Archangel Gabriel.

74 Gold agnel d'or (or mouton) of Philip IV of France (1285–1314) with the Paschal Lamb standing in front of a cross and pennon on the reverse.

us') in variously abbreviated forms. The fact that so many of the Continental coinages were issued by Church dignitaries may well account for the frequent occurrences of types of Christian significance. Many of these dignitaries themselves are found portrayed on their coins although during the early medieval period the portraits can only be said to be representational. From the fifteenth century, when realistic portraiture returned to the coinage, first in Milan and then at many other places, it became very different and the coin portrait gallery of the Popes of Rome contains many specimens of outstanding merit (**75**). Realistic portraiture was possible mainly because coins considerably larger than the grosso began to be required and struck. The extra size of the flans gave the engravers far

75 Pope Sixtus V (1585–90). During his pontificate four ancient Egyptian obelisks were found and re-erected in Rome, de-paganised and consecrated to the Christian faith by the addition of crosses to their tips.

greater scope for them to exercise their art, making more elaborate pictorial types possible.

Many cities throughout Europe featured their patron saints or their emblems as types for their coins. Examples that could be quoted include the bust or full standing figure of St Peter on the Papal coins, or a pictorial representation of him in a boat with fishing net (a type employed until very recent times), or St Mark and his lion which figured for many years on the coins of the Doges of Venice. The Florentine types of St John the Baptist and the lily were copied at a number of other mints, as mentioned earlier; in fact, it is possible to find representations on the coins of one series or another of most of the names well known in the Church calendar. One coin of this style should especially be mentioned because it is a rather strange conception. This piece, struck in Zurich early in the sixteenth century, shows the figures of Saints Felix, Regula, and Exuperantius, decapitated, each holding their head in their hands, and with a nimbus shown where their heads should have been (**76**).

The altar makes several appearances as a coin type on the coinage of ancient Rome (**25**) and during the medieval period it returned once again, but with a Christian significance. Coins

76   Large silver taler of Zurich with three decapitated saints (Felix, Regula and Exuperantius) on the obverse, each holding their heads in their hands and with a nimbus in place of their heads.

struck at Mantua include a depiction of two saints holding a monstrance over an altar which is inscribed XPR. SANGVINIS ('The Blood of Christ'), or a monstrance appears alone as the main type. As may be expected, the legends on the coins of most European mints are normally found in Latin, following the precedent established by the coinage of Rome and upon which the later coinages were founded; also, since Latin remained the universal language. The one exception to this in the English series is found on the coins of the Commonwealth (1649–60) where the legends are found in English instead of Latin and read THE COMMONWEALTH OF ENGLAND on the obverse, and GOD WITH US on the reverse (**77**).

One further group of issues should be mentioned – the coins of the Crusaders in the various kingdoms, principalities and dukedoms they established during the period. Following the general tradition of European coinages at the end of the eleventh century, when the first Crusade commenced, the coins were largely silver deniers (pennies) although struck mainly in base quality metal. A few coins appeared struck in copper. As the Crusades were in the nature of a holy war against the infidels, Christian influences can be found in the types selected for the coins, many of which exhibit the cross in one form or another. The enthroned figure of Christ appears, again following the Byzantine tradition. A number of the early

77 Silver shilling of the commonwealth of England (1649–60) with legends in English instead of the previous customary Latin, and retained in part from the Restoration to the present day.

78   Reverse of a silver denier of the Latin Kingdom of Jerusalem struck by Baldwin III (1143–63), with a representation of the Holy Sepulchre.

issues were based upon the contemporary French denier tournois with the representation of the abbey of St Martin at Tours, but what is probably the most interesting type is a representation of the Holy Sepulchre in Jerusalem (**78**), although it is little more than a conventional design. Towards the end of the period a few coins of larger size appeared, these included pieces struck by the kings of Cyprus which exhibited the Lion of Cyprus and the Jerusalem cross, and by the Knights of Rhodes, on which the Master of the Order is depicted kneeling before a cross.

The Knights of St John of Jerusalem moved their headquarters to Cyprus in 1291 when the Saracens recaptured the Holy Land, later moving on to Rhodes and finally to Malta. Coins of the Knights are found from about 1307 to 1798 and, naturally, the patron saint, St John, appears as a type shown standing, or just his head on a charger (**79**). Other coins depict the Grand Master kneeling before a cross, the Paschal Lamb and, of course, the eight-pointed-cross of the Order.

79   Silver 4-tari piece of the knights of St John of Jerusalem with the head of John the Baptist on a charger (dish).

7

MODERN TIMES

With the different series of coinages, which together extend over a period of some 2500 years, open for the consideration of the numismatist, the issues of the last few centuries are considered as 'modern'. From the sixteenth century various types of machinery have been employed to a considerable extent to assist in the production and striking of the coins. The resultant pieces have been much influenced by these methods and have become much more regular in style, thereby losing much of the individualism and delicate treatment to be found in many examples of the earlier hammered coinages.

Even in these modern issues Christian influence can still be found. In Britain, George I added to his titles on his coins FIDEI DEFENSOR ('Defender of the Faith'), although all the sovereigns from Henry VIII could have employed this had they so desired. St George, the patron saint of England, did appear briefly on the gold coins of Henry VIII, but the type was not used again until it appeared on the gold sovereigns struck by George III in 1817 (which replaced the earlier guineas which had been coined from the time of Charles II), and also on silver crown pieces issued the following year. Pistrucci's design shows St George on horseback attacking the dragon (**80**) and the design continued in use, most recently occurring on the crown piece struck

80 Benedetto Pistrucci's classic design of St George and the dragon on the reverse of a sovereign of George III.

in 1951 for the Festival of Britain and the gold sovereigns of Elizabeth II. An unusual interpretation of St George and the dragon appeared as the reverse type of the crown piece struck in 1935 to commemorate the Silver Jubilee of the reign of King George V (**81**). This was given a more modernistic treatment, which possibly is not so pleasing as the more traditional design of Pistrucci.

Although an Irish coinage is known from the eleventh century AD, the first coin of note with Christian significance is a copper half-farthing struck under King Henry VI (1422–61) which has the name of St Patrick around an open crown as the type, and then Edward IV in 1463 introduced copper farthings with a facing portrait of the saint shown wearing a mitre. These coins anticipate the introduction of a copper coinage in England by a long period. After the restoration of Charles II copper coins were struck, probably in 1678; this coinage

81 Percy Metcalfe's modernistic interpretation of St George and the dragon on George V's Silver Jubilee crown of 1935.

consisted of halfpennies which depicted St Patrick preaching to a group of people and, on the reverse, the kneeling figure of King David playing his harp, i.e. the arms of Dublin. On the companion farthings, St Patrick is shown driving the snakes out of Ireland and behind his standing figure is a church (**82**). King David is again the reverse type.

Portraits of a number of saints occur on the coinages of various parts of Europe. One of the most notable examples in recent years is that of St Stephen on a silver coin struck in Hungary in 1938 to commemorate the 900th anniversary of his death. St Peter and St Paul are both found portrayed on recent issues from the Vatican City and, as is to be expected, most other coin types from that source are of a strongly Christian character. Christian churches are still to be found: the Karls-kirche in Vienna on an Austrian coin of 1937 is an example and another fine design from the same country is the Madonna of Maria Zell. Finally, on many coins of the United States of America, a Christian declaration of faith can be found in the words IN GOD WE TRUST, which have been used from the middle of the nineteenth century onwards.

Although, strictly speaking, they are not coins, token coinages issued other than by a state authority have played an important role in the history of currency in Britain and elsewhere. In Britain during the seventeenth century there was a shortage of regal coins of low denomination which was a very considerable inconvenience to everyday trading, the situation being particularly difficult for the housewives who

82 'St Patrick's coinage' farthing with the saint carrying his patriarchal cross and driving away the reptiles on the obverse and King David playing his harp on the reverse.

needed farthings for their normal purchases. Token farthings struck in copper were introduced during the reign of James I and Charles I but for various reasons they were not popular and they failed to alleviate the situation. This led to various local authorities and others in positions of control taking matters into their own hands and, together with trades people – some 10,000 of them – striking and issuing vast numbers of tokens of copper or brass between the years 1649 and 1672. These tokens were mainly farthings, the denomination most required by the housewives, but a number of halfpennies and a few pennies also appeared; although actually illegal, the tokens served a very useful purpose to facilitate trade.

The types of the vast number of tokens issued by the trades people are extremely varied and the inscriptions generally included the name of the issuer or his initials and, if a married man, sometimes the initial of his wife's Christian name. Normally the place of issue was included with, occasionally, the street in which his place of business was situated. The spelling of the names of the towns and villages varied to a great extent and some spellings are of interest and even amusement, for example GODALLMINGE and GODLYMAN for Godalming, and PEETERBOVROWGH for Peterborough. The nature of the trade was stated clearly at times but in some instances this was made evident or implied by the types. Amongst the vast array of those that are to be found, types with a Christian connection are the Paschal Lamb, the Virgin Mary, the head of St John the Baptist on a charger, and a number of other saints including Agnes, Alban, Christopher, Clement, Dunstan, George, Lawrence, Martin, Patrick, Paul, and Peter. Representations of a church and chapel also appear. Many of these types would have represented inn signs or were a play on the name of the issuer of the token or his place of business. Similarly, they are sometimes in the nature of a trade sign as, for example, the serpent offering an apple to Eve and Adam – for a fruit seller; or the Bible which was often used as the trade sign of booksellers. One such token with the Bible as the type issued in Peterborough, probably by a Robert Benison, has for the reverse legend FEARE GOD HONOR THE KING, which legend appears also on other pieces.

Tokens of this series were also issued by townships and other authorities in addition to the trades people, simply for the benefit of all, particularly the poorer folk. Amongst these various authorities tokens were issued by mayors, constables, bailiffs, overseers for the poor, and churchwardens. One token was issued by Joseph Sayer of Newbury who was rector from 1663 to 1675; appropriately, the type of his token was a Bible (**83**).

83   Seventeenth century copper farthing token of Joseph Sayer, rector of Newbury, Berkshire, 1663 to 1675, who appropriately had a Bible represented on the reverse.

In 1672 the striking of regal copper halfpennies and farthings brought the issue of the tokens to an end for the time being, but tokens were once again issued in 1787, occasioned by the same reason as the seventeenth century issues – a shortage of regal coins of low value. To meet the requirements of trading at that time, tokens of a higher denomination were necessary and accordingly the bulk of the eighteenth century tokens were halfpennies, but with some pennies and a few farthings. Since the earlier token issues a considerable advance had been made in the engraving of the dies and in the striking processes and the eighteenth century tokens are therefore far more 'modern' in nature and appearance. The variety of types to be found is exceptionally wide and pictorial types of one sort or another are normal, and the names and places of business of the issuers are frequently found inscribed on the edges of the tokens and not on the faces. As they became so widely used and as the variation in types was so widespread, it was not long before numbers of people began to collect them and, to supplement the numbers of tokens available, certain people took advantage of this demand to produce many additional pieces which were struck to attract collectors rather than for the necessities of

84   Copper penny token, 1797, with a view of St Andrew's Church, Chesterton, Cambridge.

trading. Once again Christianity had an effect upon the selection of some of the types, but of these possibly the most interesting are the varied representations of cathedrals, churches, and chapels throughout the country (**84**). Some of them are of considerable importance as historic records as many of the original buildings depicted are no longer standing. Most of these tokens were struck before 1797 when a fresh issue of regal copper coins appeared, but a few were struck in the early years of the nineteenth century and a further issue, which included many in silver, was made between 1811 and 1817 and concluded the token coinage.

In this book consideration has been given to the use of Christian symbolism and references on the coins of Christian states following the gradual changes wrought in the Roman empire by the conversion of Constantine the Great but, as a tailpiece, an example can be quoted of what may be Christian symbolism appearing on a coin of a non-Christian ruler (**85**). The coin in question was struck in 1846 by the Sikh ruler of Kashmir, Gulab Singh, and the story of the coin, of which two versions exist, is of some interest. One version records that Gulab Singh was sitting one day talking with the British resident, Sir Henry Lawrence. The latter, as usual, was busy with numerous papers and was not giving his friend his undivided attention. Presently Gulab Singh asked Lawrence 'Why is it that in the end the English always conquer, even though at first all goes against them?' Lawrence, busy and preoccupied, reached over to a piece of paper and wrote the

85   Silver rupee of Gulab Singh of Kashmir struck in 1846 with
the letters IHS in the centre of the inscription.

letters I.H.S. These letters stand for IESUS HOMINUM SALVATOR
('Jesus, the Saviour of men') although they were originally
I.H.C. the first three letters of the name of Jesus in Greek. Gulab
Singh pondered deeply over this and ultimately decided that
the letters were some form of magic that brought power and
victory to those who used them and thus, when his next coins
were issued, he had the magic letters stamped upon them in the
hope that they would ensure lasting success in all his undertak-
ings. The alternative version of the reason why these letters are
to be found on the coins of Gulab Singh reaches a similar
conclusion, but it arrives there by rather different means. The
letters I.H.S. are also to be found on coins of Geneva where the
Christian significance attached to them would be fully understood and appreciated by the users, as opposed to those for
whom the Kashmir coins would be normal currency.

An attempt has been made throughout this book to illustrate
the many ways in which Christianity has made its mark on the
coinages issued during the Christian era. So accustomed have
people become to the use of Christian connections with coin
types and inscriptions in one manner or another that when, in
1849, Queen Victoria struck a new denomination – the silver
florin – and the titles DEI GRATIA and FIDEI DEFENSOR were
omitted from the inscription, an outcry was raised against
the coins and they have become known as the 'Godless' or
'graceless' florins. The outcry was so great that the coins
were promptly withdrawn from production and replaced in
1851 by pieces of a different design on which the omission of
the titles was rectified. This provides the clearest possible
indication of the way in which coins and Christianity have
become inseparably linked both in the British Isles and in many
other countries.

BIBLIOGRAPHY

Below are lists of books and shorter articles which have been most frequently consulted, together with others which can be suggested for further study and information on the subjects discussed. In addition to those listed, many very important articles are to be found in the pages of *The Numismatic Chronicle* (Ref. *NC*); *The British Numismatic Journal* (Ref. *BNJ*); *Coin and Medal Bulletin* (B.A. Seaby Ltd., London. – Ref. *SCMB*); *Numismatic Circular* (Spink & Son Ltd., London. – Ref. *SNC*).

GENERAL

Allbright, W. F. *The Archaeology of Palestine*. Harmondsworth, 1949.

Biggs, W. W. *An Introduction to the History of the Christian Church*. London, 1965.

British and Foreign Bible Society. Η ΚΑΙΝΗ ΔΙΑΘΗΚΗ. 2nd ed. London, 1958.

Caiger, S. L. *Archaeology and the New Testament*. London, 1939.

Clogg, F. B. *An Introduction to the New Testament*. 2nd ed. London, 1940.

Finegan, J. *Light from the Ancient Past*. Princeton, 1946.

Finley, M. I. *The Ancient Greeks*. Harmondsworth, 1966.

Grierson, P. *Numismatics*. Oxford, 1975.

Keller, W. *The Bible as History*. Rev. ed. London, 1958.

Perowne, S. *The Later Herods*. London, 1965.

— *Caesars and Saints*. London, 1962.

Redlich, E. B. *The Student's Introduction to the Synoptic Gospels*. London, 1936.

Sutherland, C. H. V. *Art in Coinage*. London and New York, 1956.

Wegener, G. S. *6000 Years of the Bible*. London, 1958.

Weymouth, R. F. *New Testament in Modern Speech*. 3rd ed. London, 1952.

Wilson, I. *Jesus: The Evidence*. London, 1984.

CHAPTERS 1 TO 3

Alfoldi, A. *The Conversion of Constantine and Pagan Rome*. Oxford, 1948.

Anon. *The Coins of Axum*. *SCMB* 1960.

Carson, R. A. G., Hill, P. V., and Kent, J. P. C. *Late Roman Bronze Coinage*. London, 1960.

Hart, H. St.J. 'Judaea and Rome. The Official Commentary', *Journal of Theological Studies*. (Oxford), Oct. 1952.

Head, B. V. *Historia Numorum*. London, 1911; reprinted 1963.

Hill, G. F. *Catalogue of the Greek Coins in the British Museum*. *Palestine*. London, 1914, reprinted.

— *The Medallic Portraits of Christ – The False Shekels – The Thirty Pieces of Silver*. Oxford, 1920.

Lessen, M. Van. 'The Coinage of Palestine in the First and Second Centuries A.D.', *SNC* 1971.

Mattingly, H. *Roman Coins*. London, 2nd ed. 1962.

Mattingly, H., Sydenham, E. A. *et al*. *Roman Imperial Coinage*. 9 vols. London, 1923 onwards and reprints.

Meshorer, Y. *Jewish Coins of the Second Temple Period*. Tel-Aviv, 1967.

Reifenberg, A. *Israel's History in the Coins of the Maccabees to the Roman Conquest*. London, 1953.

— *Jewish Coins*. 4th ed. Jerusalem, 1965.

Ridgeway, W. *The Origins of Metallic Currency and Weight Standards*. London, 1892, reprinted 1976.

Price, M. *Coins of the Bible*. London, 1975.

Scrase, D. *Coins of Bible Days*.   Booklets accompanying 12 slides
— *Coins of the Jews*.   published by British Museum Publi-
                                                      cations, London, 1978 and 1979.

Seaby, H. A. *Roman Silver Coins*. Vol. 1: *Republic to Augustus*. 3rd ed.
        revised by D. R. Sear and R. Loosley. London, 1978.
— *Roman Silver Coins*. Vol. 2: *Tiberius to Commodus*. 3rd ed. revised
        by R. Loosley. London, 1979.

Sear, D. R. *Greek Coins and Their Values*. Vol. 1: *Europe*. London,
        1978.
— *Greek Coins and Their Values*. Vol. 2: *Asia and Africa*. London,
        1979.
— *Roman Coins and Their Values*. 3rd rev. ed. London, 1981.
— *Byzantine Coins and Their Values*. London, 1974.

Seltman, C. T. *Greek Coins*. 2nd ed. London, 1966.

Sydenham, E. A. *Coinage of the Roman Republic*. London, 1952.

Wacks, M. 'Ezekiel's Vision', *SNC* 1976.

Yadin, Y. *Bar Kochba*. London, 1971.

CHAPTERS 4 TO 7

Bedoukian, P. Z. *Coinage of Cilician Armenia*. New York, 1962.

Blunt, C. E., Lyon, C. S. S., and Stewart, B. H. I. H. 'The Coinage
        of Southern England 796–840', *BNJ* XXXII (1963).

Brooke, G. C. *English Coins*. London, 1932, 2nd ed. reprinted 1966.

Brown, C. J. *The Coins of India*. London, 1922.

Brown, I. D. 'The King's Evil', *SCMB* 1956.

Dalton, R., and Hamer, S. H. *The Provincial Token Coinage of the
        Eighteenth Century*. 1910–1918, reprinted 1977.

Dowle, P., and Finn, P. *The Guide Book to the Coinage of Ireland from
        995 AD to the Present Day*. London, 1969.

Grierson, P. 'The Canterbury (St. Martin's) Hoard of Frankish and
        Anglo-Saxon Coin-Ornaments', *BNJ* XXVII (1958).

Hazlitt, W. *The Coinage of the European Continent*. London, 1897,
        reprinted 1974.

Jacob, K. A. 'The Coins of Cilician Armenia', *SCMB* 1976.

Mitchener, M. *Oriental Coins and Their Values*:
— Vol. 1. *The World of Islam*. London, 1977.
— Vol. 2. *The Ancient and Classical World*. London, 1978.

— Vol. 3. *Non-Islamic and Colonial Coinage*. London, 1979.

North, J. J. *English Hammered Coinage*. Vol. 1 Rev. ed. London, 1980.

— Vol. 2 Rev. ed. London, 1976.

Oman, C. *The Coinage of England*. London, 1931, reprinted 1976.

Purvey, P. F. *Coins and Tokens of Scotland*. London, 1970.

Seaby. *Standard Catalogue of British Coins*. Vol. 1: *Coins of England and the United Kingdom*. 21st ed. London, 1985.

— *Standard Catalogue of British Coins*. Vol. 2: *Coins of Scotland, Ireland and the Islands*. London, 1984.

Seaby, P. *Coins and Tokens of Ireland*. London, 1972.

Stewart, I. H. *The Scottish Coinage*, with supplement. London, 1955.

Williamson, G. C. *Trade Tokens Issued in the Seventeenth Century*. London 1889/91, reprinted, 3 vols. 1967.

Woolf, N. 'The Sovereign Remedy: Touch-Pieces and the King's Evil', *BNJ* XLIX.

INDEX OF
BIBLICAL REFERENCES

96